*Twayne's United States Authors Series*

Sylvia E. Bowman, *Editor*

INDIANA UNIVERSITY

*E. B. White*

# E. B. WHITE

By EDWARD C. SAMPSON

*State University of New York
College at Oneonta*

 232

Twayne Publishers, Inc.   ::   New York

Library of Congress Cataloging in Publication Data

Sampson, Edward C.
    E. B. White.

    (Twayne's United States author series, TUSAS 232)
    Bibliography:   p.
    1. White, Elwyn Brooks, 1899-            —Criticism and
interpretation.
PS3545.H5187Z9            818'.5'209            73-21582
ISBN 0-8057-0787-5

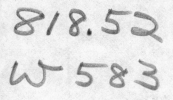
To
SUSAN AND NED

# Preface

E. B. White has been the spokesman for a sturdy minority —for those who have principles yet avoid labels; who like clarity of thought and reject cant; and who, because they respect and seek privacy, may be a vanishing or obsolescent breed. His own summation of his life, paraphrasing Max Beerbohm, was that he had had a nice little career. But we, at least the members of that minority, being under no obligation to accept his modest assessment, can rank him as one of America's distinguished men of letters.

My intention in this study—the first on E. B. White—is to present him both as a commentator on the American scene and as a literary artist. I have made no attempt to discuss everything that he wrote; those pieces that have seemed to me important have received, naturally, the most attention. I have tried to let White speak for himself as much as possible, and therefore have quoted extensively from his writing—I hope not excessively. As one of our most polished writers, his own words often reveal more than any amount of commentary.

A sizeable portion of White's writing remains uncollected: for example, from the late 1920's until 1937, he contributed a large share of the weekly "Notes and Comment" department of *The New Yorker*, but only a part of this work has been reprinted. However, his best work, including some of those contributions, *has* been reprinted—many times in some cases, for White has been represented in a multitude of college anthologies. With the exception of *One Man's Meat* and his children's stories, the major portion of his work appeared first in *The New Yorker*.

I discuss most of White's work chronologically, generally in terms of the publication date of collections of his work where his writing is now most easily available. The approach has made sense to me, although it may need some further explanation. Except for his three children's stories, White has been above all a writer of his times, an interpreter of the contemporary scene; and, as such, it has seemed not only wise but necessary to consider his writing against the changing background of his times: the 1920's, the Depression, the challenge of Fascism, World War II, the cold war, and the atomic age. The alternative—to deal with White the humorist, the internationalist, the skeptic, and so on—seemed wrong. But I have made two exceptions to the chronological approach: I have considered most of White's poetry in Chapter II, and I have discussed his three children's stories in a single chapter.

I am grateful to many people for their help in this work. Dale Mitchell and Howard Cushman remembered many useful things about White's Cornell University days and the years immediately afterward. Philip O'Connor, Lewis Weeks, and Robert Levine read parts of my manuscript and made valuable suggestions. I owe a special word of thanks to my nephew, Martin W. Sampson III, who spurred me on to this work in the first place by himself writing of E. B. White (his essay won a prize at the Hotchkiss School), and who dug out for me hard-to-find material about White at Cornell. I am grateful to Frances H. Sampson for her careful reading of the whole manuscript, and to John Cranford Adams, who has saved me from many a foolish sentence. Charles Penrose of the Clarkson College Library arranged innumerable interlibrary loans and was otherwise helpful. Ebba Jonsson of *The New Yorker* staff has assisted me in every way she could, and the late Professor George Healey put the E. B. White collection at Cornell at my disposal. Above all, I am grateful to E. B. White himself for patiently answering my questions, giving me permission to quote from his manuscripts at Cornell, and for reading my manuscript and making many helpful comments. None of these people, of course, can bear any responsibility for the weaknesses that remain in my book. At the last, a quiet word of thanks to my wife, Cynthia.

## Preface

I acknowledge with thanks permission from Harper and
Row to quote from *Charlotte's Web, Every Day Is Saturday, The Fox of Peapack, Here Is New York, Is Sex Necessary?, The Lady Is Cold, One Man's Meat, The Points of My
Compass, Quo Vadimus?, The Second Tree from the Corner,* and *Stuart Little*; from Little, Brown and Company to
quote from James Thurber's *The Years with Ross*; from The
Macmillan Company to quote from William Strunk and E. B.
White, *The Elements of Style*; from *The New Yorker* to
quote from various uncollected contributions by E. B.
White; from E. B. White permission to quote from *A Subtreasury of American Humor* and *The Wild Flag;* and from
the Cornell Alumni Association to quote from *Our Cornell.*

I have usually indicated page numbers of quotations in
the text. But, when the quotations have come from pieces
by White of only a few pages in length, and when the piece
can easily be found by its title, I have omitted cluttering the
text with references.

EDWARD C. SAMPSON

# Contents

# Chronology

1899    Elwyn Brooks White, born July 11 in Mount Vernon,
        New York; son of Jessie Hart White and Samuel T.
        White, head of Waters Piano Company, New York,
        New York.

1913-   Attended Mount Vernon High School; published
1917    poems, essays, short stories in the Mount Vernon
        High School *Oracle*.

1917    Served in the Farm Cadets in Hempstead, Long
        Island; entered Cornell University.

1918    Registered for the draft in September; enlisted as a
        private in the Student Army Training Corps at Cor-
        nell.

1920-   Editor-in-chief of the *Cornell Daily Sun*; won first
1921    prize for an editorial submitted to the Convention
        of Eastern College Newspapers, an award made by
        Arthur Brisbane. Editorial, "The King's English,"
        published in the *Sun*, May 18, 1920.

1921    Graduated from Cornell University; declined offer of
        a teaching position at the University of Minnesota.

1921-   Brief jobs with the United Press; with the house
1922    organ of a silk mill; and with the American Legion
        News Service.

1922    Across the country in his Model T Ford, *Hotspur*,
        with Howard Cushman; May 14, published a sonnet
        "To Morvich, Winner" in the *Louisville Herald*
        (Morvich won the Kentucky Derby that year).

1922-  September-June, reporter and columnist on the
1923   *Seattle Times*; summer 1923, trip to Alaska in the
       *Buford.*

1923-  Lived with three other Cornellians at 112 West 13th
1924   Street, New York, New York. "I spent a solid year
       once experimenting with idleness and finding out
       exactly what it was like to occupy myself with
       nothing at all over a wide range of the country."

1924   Worked for Frank Seaman, Inc., advertising; occa-
       sional jobs as usher at the Metropolitan Opera; pub-
       lished poems in "The Conning Tower."

1925   Worked for J. H. Newmark, advertising; published
       his first piece "Defense of the Bronx River" in
       *The New Yorker.*

1926   Trip abroad, paid for by Cunard in return for his writ-
       ing the script of a promotional film advertising
       College Cabin Class; began working part-time for
       *The New Yorker.*

1927-  Full-time on *The New Yorker;* wrote a considerable
1938   part of "Notes and Comment," as well as poems,
       sketches, short stories, newsbreaks, picture captions,
       and reviews.

1928-  Took part during the summer in operating Camp
1929   Otter, a boys' camp in Ontario; White part-owner.

1929   *The Lady Is Cold; Is Sex Necessary?* (written with
       James Thurber); married to Katharine S. Angell.

1930   Son Joel born.

1931   *Ho-Hum: Newsbreaks from The New Yorker.*

1932   *Another Ho-Hum.*

1934   *Every Day Is Saturday.*

1936   *Farewell to Model T* (with Richard Lee Strout: pub-
       lished under the name of Lee Strout White).

## Chronology

1938    *The Fox of Peapack and Other Poems*; left New York to live on his farm in Maine; began contributions to "One Man's Meat" in *Harper's*.

1939    *Quo Vadimus?*

1941    Edited, with Katharine S. White, *A Subtreasury of American Humor*.

1942    *One Man's Meat*; resumed active participation on *The New Yorker*.

1944    Enlarged edition of *One Man's Meat*.

1945    Reporter at large for *The New Yorker* to cover the San Francisco Conference—the beginnings of the United Nations; *Stuart Little*.

1946    *The Wild Flag*.

1948    Honorary degrees from Dartmouth College, University of Maine, and Yale University.

1949    *Here Is New York*.

1950    Honorary degree from Bowdoin College.

1952    *Charlotte's Web*; honorary degree from Hamilton College.

1954    *The Second Tree from the Corner*; honorary degrees from Harvard University and Colby College; received the Page One Award for Literature from Newspaper Guild of New York for *The Second Tree from the Corner*.

1957    Gave up New York apartment and resumed year-round residence in Maine.

1959    Edited, and added a chapter to, *The Elements of Style* by William Strunk, Jr.

1960    Received the Gold Medal for Essays and Criticism from the National Institute of Arts and Letters.

1962 *The Points of My Compass.*

1963 Received the Presidential Medal of Freedom.

1970 Received the Laura Ingalls Wilder Medal for his contribution to literature for children; *The Trumpet of the Swan.*

1971 Received the National Medal for Literature.

*E. B. White*

CHAPTER *1*

# "The Years of Wonder"

## I  *Cornell*

IN "I'd Send My Son to Cornell" E. B. White wrote that the most romantic journey of his life was the last lap of the trip from New York to Ithaca, the run on the spur line of the Delaware, Lackawanna & Western that took him from Owego through the valley of the Catatonk, through "Candor, Willseyville, Caroline, where September lies curled up asleep in every pasture and life lies curled up in the towers at the end of the line" (12). His destination in the fall of 1917 was Cornell University.

Surely, White would have been a writer had he never gone to Cornell. He remembers publishing something—a poem, he thinks—around 1910 in *The Ladies' Home Journal*; he won a book for a prize: *Rab and His Friends*.[1] Barrett Brady, a friend of White, recalls two school-boy poems, one of them a comic valentine in verse to their algebra teacher;[2] he published "A True Dog Story" in *St. Nicholas* in 1914;[3] and, as he told Roderick Nordell, he was a "writing fool in high school," contributing, for example, a number of items to the Mt. Vernon High School *Oracle* (he was also class artist).[4] Yet the particular quality of Cornell had something to do with the direction that White's gifts took him. The beauty of the setting, the intellectual activity, the cosmopolitan student body, the blend of the theoretical and the practical like the engineers surveying on the arts quadrangle—all these were important. At Cornell, wrote White,

I knew two men from Hawaii, a girl from Johannesburg, a Cuban, a Turk, an Englishman from India, a Negro from New York, two farmers, three Swedes, a Quaker, five Southerners, a reindeer

butcher, a second lieutenant, a Christian Scientist, a retired
dancer, a motorcyclist, a man who had known Theda Bara, three
gnomes, and a lutist. That's not counting the general run of
broad-jumpers, second tenors, and veterinarians who make up
the great body of undergraduates, the same as in any school.
("I'd Send My Son to Cornell," 13)


White came to college at a troubled time. Toward the end
of his senior year at Mount Vernon High School, he began
to record in his journal (he quotes from it in *One Man's
Meat*) some of his growing awareness of world problems:
"The country is at war and I think I ought to serve (110)."
He could write poetry, he could play the piano, and he was
thinking about summer canoe trips; but he suffered from the
guilty restlessness that any young man might have felt in
the summer of 1917: "My birthday!" he wrote on July 11,
1917. "Eighteen, and still no future! I'd be more contented
in prison, for there at least I would know precisely what
I had to look forward to (111)." In one of the manuscript
versions of "Zoo Revisited," he had written: "What were
the questions in those days? Life, love, war, girls . . . ."
    Though White was lonely and homesick when he first
arrived at college, Cornell gave him some sense of purpose. He took long walks, seemed to enjoy his introductory
course in literature (English 3), and began to see some of
his professors socially—something a little unusual for a
freshman. He mentions being taken to the house of Professor Bristow Adams: "I got a good deal out of the com-
panionship of an older man who was a faculty member and
having his family there, because this was like having a
second home."⁵ Later, he became acquainted with two
other professors at Cornell who had a strong influence on
him: Martin W. Sampson and William S. Strunk, Jr. "But
those were the things, those three professors . . . . They
were a great trio."⁶
    In addition, White made the board of the *Cornell Daily
Sun,* a real accomplishment for a freshman. He was on the
*Sun* for the rest of his college days. The war, however, was
still very much with him: "Shall I set out," he asked himself in his journal toward the end of his freshman year, "to

fit myself for some branch of the service so that at the age
of 21 I will be trained in military or war work, or shall I wait
still longer in the hope that peace will come?" *(One
Man's Meat,* 113).

The draft helped solve the problem. White registered
on September 12, 1918, and on returning to Cornell for his
sophomore year enlisted as a private in the Students' Army
Training Corps. He took courses in both academic and military subjects; at the completion of his military training,
he would be pulled out of college and remain in the army
presumably for the duration of the war. Part of the army,
the Students' Army Training Corps was a full-scale affair:
in all, 1790 students were enrolled in the corps at Cornell.[7]
The war ended in November 1918; by December White had
returned to the curriculum of an English major, and the
*Sun,* which had closed down briefly, resumed publication.

E. B. White was an active student; the 1921 *Cornellian*
has five lines of credits under his name, one of the longest
entries in the year-book.[8] He took a wide variety of English
courses, including Nineteenth Century Poetry, Dramatic
Structure, Modern Novelists, Shakespeare, the Art of Poetry,
the History of English Literature, American Literature,
and English 8, Usage and Style, given by William Strunk.

The English Department in White's years at Cornell was
distinguished. In addition to Sampson and Strunk, there
were, among others, Joseph Q. Adams, Frederick C. Pres-
cott, and Lane Cooper. Although too much should not be
made of White's formal education, his acquaintance with
English literature, besides the usual values we can assume,
gave him material later on for serious poetry and for parody.
Even in class White's wit was evident. When Professor
Strunk, in his survey course in English literature, had begun to read from "The Blessed Damozel" the lines "The
blessed damozel leaned out/From the gold bar of heaven"
White commented out loud, "I'm glad to know there is a bar
in heaven."[9]

In addition to his class work in English, White was an
active member of the Manuscript Club, a group that met
at the house of Martin Sampson, read creative works to one
another, and criticized them freely. A lively group, it in-

cluded William Strunk, sometimes Bristow Adams, and nine or ten students. Among other things, White gained experience in writing in a number of different poetic forms, including at least one "penitential sonnet"[10] without the letter "h." Entitled "To My Dog, Leaving Me," it ended "As, 'gainst your epidermis, clings a flea, /So, dog, may you in spirit cling to me."

Though the members of the club wrote in many different forms, the sonnet was their official medium. We may suppose that, in writing that short and disciplined form, White was learning the art of the short and pithy observation—the art he later put to such good use in *The New Yorker*. White wrote an article on the Manuscript Club for the *Cornell Era,* and in it he stated the creed of the club as formulated by Professor Sampson: "To be frank, to use one's brains, to write what is in one to write, and never to take oneself too damned seriously or too damned lightly."[11] This was not exactly White's creed, or *The New Yorker's* (if such exists), yet we can see traces of the attitude throughout White's writing.

Important as his courses and his membership in the Manuscript Club may have been to White, his work on the *Cornell Daily Sun* probably influenced him most during his Cornell years. He had been on the *Sun* since his freshman year; had written some editorials (signed E. B. W.) his junior year; and on April 5, 1920, he became its editor-in-chief. From then until April 5, 1921, the end of his senior year, he wrote most of the *Sun* editorials. Many of the editorials dealt with usual college issues. White, concerned about the status of probation, questioned some of the penalties associated with it; he supported the athletic teams, particularly crew and track, which were then in their glory at Cornell; he was all for college spirit, and advised the freshmen to maintain the Cornell traditions; he argued for the honor system; and he recommended that more tennis courts be built.

But there were some more serious comments. White argued eloquently for the establishment of a school of journalism at Cornell; he regretted that a track meet between Harvard and Virginia had been cancelled because the Harvard team had two Negroes: it might have been a chance, he wrote, for Virginia "to cast off for the moment any inherent territorial prejudices (January 18, 1921)." He also commented on the case of a teacher in Buffalo who had been dismissed because of her "adherence to Soviet doctrine." The test, he said, was how good a teacher she was, for "Communistic beliefs would not necessarily make her a poor teacher of history or of spelling (January 20, 1921)."

White liked to enumerate his points—"first, second, third, and finally." And sometimes he slipped into such things as this: Cornell has "pretty fair traditions, pretty fine students, pretty capable professors, and is, in a word, a pretty good place (Dec. 22, 1920)." He also used "imperturbability," a word that he and James Thurber later seemed to have had a curious fondness for. On occasion, White reprinted a headline or news item, and added a comment—the beginning of what he was to do to perfection for the Newsbreak Department of *The New Yorker.* For example, after he had quoted a *New York Tribune* headline "Inaugural of Harding will be made more simple than that of Lincoln," he commented, "This seems to apply even to the man himself (January 21, 1921)."

White achieved considerable distinction for one of his editorials. On May 8, 1920, a news-item in the *Sun* announced that an editorial submitted by E. B. White to the Convention of Eastern College Newspapers was awarded first prize by Arthur Brisbane, editor of the New York *Evening Journal.* The editorial, entitled "The King's English," appeared in the *Sun* on May 18, 1920. White discussed the use of jargon by undergraduates, criticized their poor enunciation, and regretted that the resources of English were not better used. There are times, he said, when the student cannot use his vernacular, or finds it wanting: "Little delicacies of expression are entirely beyond his reach. He is unable to express the shades of meaning which are in his mind. Bereft of his one means of conveying an impression forcefully, he listens to his prattle in dismay, and marvels at its weakness and childishness. It is only in such a position that he realizes what an elusive thing a word can be, and wishes he had taken a course in public speaking—his idea of the way to learn to speak."

Through his position on the *Sun*, White was involved in several controversies. The most important, and probably from White's point of view the silliest, had to do with the two senior honorary societies at Cornell.[12] Early in May 1920, one of the societies, Quill and Dagger, published an announcement in the *Sun* that "we the undersigned senior honorary society will not consider for election to membership in the society at the annual spring [meeting] members of the junior class who are on probation." On May 10, 1920, White wrote an editorial approving in general of the new standards for Quill and Dagger membership; and he noted that the effect on scholarship in general at Cornell should be beneficial.

The other senior honorary society at Cornell, Sphinx Head, took strong exception to the editorial, feeling that it was an unfair attempt on White's part to influence his classmates in their choice of membership in either of the societies. (Both societies had earlier agreed not to extend invitations to any undergraduate who could be shown to have influenced his classmates' choice.) Therefore, Sphinx Head announced formally in the *Sun* that White would not be considered for election (normally, the editor of the *Sun* could be confident of an invitation).

Although this seems undergraduate nonsense, it had an effect on White. Years later, he said: "As you can readily see . . . I was learning about journalism fast and the hard way. What I had considered to be a theoretical, philosophical, and detached editorial . . . [was] interpreted as a sinister attempt to influence juniors. This struck me as comical, but informative." The situation reached a happy climax for White in an English class:

On the morning the Sphinx Head resolution appeared in the *Sun*, I sat down in Martin Sampson's class in Goldwin Smith. Before the lecture began, I saw Professor Sampson leave his podium. He strode, erect and silent, down the aisle toward me, paused at my desk, and deposited a slip of paper in front of me. Then he turned immediately, and returned to his place at the head of the class.

I have this slip of paper. It is pasted neatly in my journal.

Pencilled in his fine hand, it reads: 'On account of his editorial of May 10, I shall not invite E. B. White '21 to dinner.

Old Philadelphia Lady.'

I have never felt more grateful to anyone than I did to Professor Sampson on that queer morning. His reassurance was more than just friendly, it was subtle and comical, and I felt suddenly reborn.

Another controversy is worth recalling because it probably provoked White into writing a good editorial on free speech. He had been attacked in *The Critic*, a minor undergraduate publication, for "weak and vacillating" policies and for "suppression of facts and garbling of headlines."[13] The attack may have risen out of a fatuous clamor about coeds; anyway, a few days later, White published an editorial entitled "Free Speech and Bad Judgment." It reads in part:

Some thoughts may be uttered freely, and others are a bit free when uttered. Some persons speak freely and others use free speech, freely or otherwise. Which brings up the question, When is speech free?

In all ages there have been persons who have been willing to say things which other persons were accustomed to keep quiet about. In this way the world has advanced. If it were not for the willingness of certain liberty-loving individuals to break free from dogma and convention, we would be where we were thousands of years ago. The chief reason that there has been any argument at all about free speech is because the persons doing the talking often had bad judgment along with good opinions. There is a pretty fair opportunity in this country for the expression of any view, when well presented. That is why it is so unfortunate that so often the manner of speech detracts from the meaning behind it, and sentiment swings suddenly in the opposite direction. That clouds the real issue of free speech, which must forever be preserved. (Dec. 10, 1920)

Something of the clarity of the mature White is here—in the last part of the second paragraph, for example. As Morris Bishop has noted, "the rarely chastened style of his editorials is still remembered by elder members of the English Department."[14]

Whatever the coed controversy was exactly, White, years later, remembered something about it. On January 23, 1965, in one of his more recent contributions to "Notes and Comment" he spoke wryly about the changing sexual attitudes on college campuses. Princeton undergraduates, he noted, were now clamoring for coeds, but he could recall "a day in Ithaca in 1920 when a group of male undergraduates emerged from solemn conclave with the demand that coeds be banished from Cornell." White, judging from the *Sun* editorials on the subject, had no interest in seeing coeds abolished; what his own personal attachments were, it is hard to say. A poem he wrote for the Manuscript Club should tell enough for most purposes:

> If I had time I'd fall in love
>   And mope in corners:
> I'd call the stars to witness my devotion to my love
>   If I had time.
>
> O crazy hours! With what alacrity I jump
>   From toil to toil,
> Filling the days and nights with labors all concise and
>       scheduled there
>   Because I acquiesce.
>
> How quite unbroken is the daily round
>   I seem to make,
> To no great purpose—when instead I might be sighing
>       lovers' sighs
>   And writing awful verse.
>
> If I had time I'd fall in love,
>   Nor do I doubt
> With whom, you know, hi ho—nor do I doubt with whom,
>   If I had time.

At least four important points can be made about White's Cornell years: the beautiful and cosmopolitan setting stimulated his imagination; his courses brought him into contact with lively teachers and gave him a broad acquaintance with English literature; the Manuscript Club gave him the opportunity to develop his poetic style, to benefit from the criticism of others, and to gain from Professor

Sampson and Professor Strunk what Morris Bishop called
"a taste for elegant badinage."[15] Finally, the *Sun* helped
him to discover in the writing of editorials "the congenial
form which he has practiced all his life."[16]

There is little doubt that it was the *Sun* that most influenced White. Making the paper in his freshman year,
he stated, was one of the outstanding events of his college
days.[17] It was a hard job and White gave it a lot of time. When
he was night editor, he was up late, and he had a long walk
home: "My chief memory of *Sun* days is of the long and
lonely uphill walk home at two in the morning. (The last
street car ran at midnight.) There was a large cemetery
that was useful as a shortcut if you were willing to walk
through a graveyard at that hour, and I was. Those walks
have stayed with me; everything else has vanished."[18] In
his interview with Susan I. Frank, White spoke more about
the importance of Cornell and the *Sun*:

Well, Cornell elevated my spirit. I was on a high hill in more ways
than one. I was in love. Cornell also made a journalist out of me,
as distinct from a literary man, or a novelist, or a business man.
The *Sun* took almost all my time and attention. I was fascinated by the reporting and editorial writing particularly. I'm
a moralist, I guess, and I wrote editorials. I think that really
changed me—I mean, it shaped my career to have done that.[19]

## II  *Alaska*

When E. B. White graduated from Cornell, a number of
possibilities were open to him. He could have taken a
teaching position at the University of Minnesota, but as
a former editor of the *Sun*, he logically turned to journalism, taking a job with the United Press. Dale Kramer has
chronicled White's misfortunes with the United Press, and
has described two other jobs White held briefly. His tenure
with the United Press ended when he took the wrong train
and missed an assignment he was supposed to cover—the
funeral of a statesman; his job writing for a silk-factory
publication was over when he read the horoscope of a girl

employee and predicted that she would have three children
and never marry. Next, he stayed with the American Legion News Service (where, in the same building, Harold
Ross, later the editor of *The New Yorker,* was working)
long enough to earn money to buy a Model T Ford (*Ross
and The New Yorker,* 144).

With his Model T, named *Hotspur,* White began another
of the romantic journeys of his life. Restless, unsettled, he
had not found what he wanted to do, or could do well,
and it was fortunate that he was able to continue his explo-
ration of life, and of himself. He left in the spring of 1922
with a Cornell classmate, Howard Cushman, on an ex-
pedition that ended some six months later in Seattle, Washington.

The trip and its aftermath, especially White's jaunt to
Alaska, was pivotal in his development as a man and artist.
Not much, perhaps, emerged directly; an impromptu sonnet; the beautifully detailed essay on Model T Fords,
"Farewell, My Lovely!" (which he wrote nostalgically in
1936); one of his finest pieces, "The Years of Wonder"
(which appeared still later, in 1961); and a few other items.
But indirectly the trip marks the development of White's
skill as an observer of the contemporary scene, the maturing of his deep human sympathy and veneration for his
fellow man, and his growing knowledge of himself.

The two camped out some of the time, following a pattern
that, as Howard Cushman describes it,[20] must have been
hard on the stomach. They would pass through a town at
dusk, and camp a few miles beyond, as soon as they found
a good field. The next morning, instead of returning to the
town for breakfast, they would, at White's insistence, drive
on, hungry, till the next town.

The pair reached Louisville, Kentucky, in time for the
1922 Derby. White bet on the wrong horse, and wanted
to recover his losses. After dinner that day, as Howard Cushman tells the story, White parked *Hotspur* under a street
light, and with his Corona on his lap typed out the following sonnet, which he sold to the Louisville *Herald* for five
dollars. It appeared the next day on the front page:

To Morvich, Winner

Bold son of Runnymede—what tho you came
From out the East! Clean-heeled and void of fear
You met the pick of splendid horsedom here
And won—Kentucky celebrates your name.
Proud winner of the turf, the Derby fame,
Topping the laurels that from far and near
Were yours, proclaims your title free and clear—
Crowns you immortal in an ancient game.

The flying figure of a sleek brown colt
Over the downs a mellow sun revealed—
Exponent of a kingly sport. No doubt,
Then, why men thrilled to see you bolt—
Not for your birth nor for your money yield,
But that you gloriously went the route.[21]

In addition to his typewriter, White had brought along a stringed instrument of his own manufacture. As both James Thurber and Ralph Ingersoll have been somewhat vague in their descriptions of the contraption, it might be well to describe it. White had made the instrument before he left home out of a stick, a cigar box, and a single string; he played it with a worn violin bow. It hung from the windshield frame of the car, and once, near Ashland, Kentucky, a gas-station attendant asked White what it was. White offered to play a tune on it for a tank of gas; the attendant (whose name, White had noted from a sign, was O'Reilly) agreed; and there followed, as Cushman says, a "flawless 'Wearing of the Green.'"

They got to Montana. According to Ingersoll, White liked it and might have stayed had it not been for his hayfever. They went on to Seattle, and, not being able to go much farther, did stay there. With the help of a friend, White got a job in the fall of 1922 on the Seattle *Times* as a reporter at forty dollars a week.[22] White's problems on the Seattle *Times* have been variously described;[23] the best summary is the one White gave to Susan Frank: "I worked for a year on the Seattle *Times* and I discovered that I would never make a good newspaper reporter. It was out of the

question. The city editor discovered it; he knew even
before I did. I was not quick enough or alert enough—I
was always taking the wrong train going in the wrong
direction" (*Cornell Daily Sun*, S-2).

One of the more curious things that White did for the
Seattle *Times*, beginning some months after he was hired,
was to conduct a "Personal Column" which his publisher,
Colonel C. B. Blethen, contrived as a device to stimulate
the sales of his classified advertising department. White
described the column and his duties:

[Blethen] named the column "Personal Column," ordered it
set in the style of classified ads, and directed it to be run *in* the
classified section, where, of course, it was almost indistinguishable
from the ads themselves. He scrapped the first column I turned
in and wrote one himself, which ran on Page 1. For a couple of
days thereafter he continued to supervise the thing, and then
left me alone with my queer baby. Most of the readers of the *Times*,
I think, never knew of the existence of the Personal Column. As
for me, I was pleased to have an outlet for poems and paragraphs,
no matter how odd its format. . . . One or two of my standard
headings were the forerunners of *New Yorker* newsbreak heads—
"Answers to Hard Questions" was one.[24]

The column must have taken a good bit of time; White had
to report for work at seven in the morning. The column,
written mostly in the style of humor White had been familiar with on the *Sun*, was hard work. Two examples
follow:

*We Answer Hard Questions*

Sir: What happens to prune pits?
L. N. Q. They seek their own level.

I don't know what "L. N. Q." meant, but White often used
initials in the imaginary items he put in the column. (The
ones who might know are the readers of the "Berry Patch"
in the *Sun* of White's day, where odd names and initials
like X. L. C. Orr and Lucinda Beene turned up). The other
example:

Professional

---

Sir: We have a very stupid family physician. He thinks a counter-irritant is a lady who puts her vanity case next to a man's soup at a short order lunch counter. W. J. R.

---

Wonder if he thinks an Indian club has by-laws?[25]

It is hard to see how White kept writing this sort of thing as long as he did. He has noted that so far as he remembered, he wrote the column until he was dropped from the *Times* in June 1923. The editor commented that the dismissal was "no reflection" on White's ability *(The Points of My Compass,* 206). At any rate, in "Speaking of Counterweights," White looked back on his Seattle experience with a nostalgic pleasure, as well as with a sense of his unfitness for the life.

One of the most dramatic events of those unsettled years was White's journey to Alaska in the steamer *Buford.* He was, he said, "rather young to be going so far north, but there is a period near the beginning of every man's life when he has little to cling to except his unmanageable dream, little to support him except good health, and nowhere to go but all over the place. This period in my life lasted about eight years, and I spent the summer of one of those years in and around Alaska" *(The Points of My Compass,* 205). There is no need to recount here the details of the trip, for White has recorded many of these in "The Years of Wonder." What he hasn't recorded, though, was that the *Buford,* which had been an army transport, had been used in 1919 to transport "radicals" to Russia. The press had christened her *The Soviet Ark.* [26]

The most dramatic event of the voyage was White's change in status from first-class passenger to saloonsman, and then to firemen's messboy. As a saloonsman, White felt he belonged to the ship: "No longer was the *Buford* merely taking me from one benighted port to another; now she was transporting me from all my yesterdays to all my tomorrows" *(The Points of My Compass,* 219). White apparently found in this trip something of what he had been looking for. One of the reasons Alaska attracted him, he said, was that it was "in the opposite direction from home, where I considered it unsuitable to be at my age" (208). He welcomed the shift from passenger to crew member: he wanted to make his way "farther down in the ship, sink to the depths, and try the rapture of human dereliction and drudgery" (223).

During her voyage, the *Buford* stopped at Dutch Harbor, near Unalaska. Though less dramatic than his change in status, the stop had a curious significance for White. In "This Is a Prayer Before I Sleep," a poem published later in *The Lady Is Cold* (1929), he wrote:

> And once, in a ship, in a frozen sea,
> I glimpsed a thing that was really me.
> In at the death
> Let me draw the same courageous breath
> I drew the day I looked on Unalaska.

In "The Years of Wonder," White is more explicit; nearly forty years later perhaps he could see things more clearly: "By some standards, the place could have been called dead, but, walking the length of Unalaska at the foot of the green, tumbled hills, alone and wonder-struck, I felt more alive than I had ever felt before in my life. I was about as far west as a man could conveniently get on this continent, I was a long, long way from home, songs of praise knocked in my head, and I felt a gush of exhilaration" (*The Points of My Compass*, 224).

After Unalaska, White's job changed again—this time to firemen's messboy—"the true beginning of the voyage for me," he wrote. He continued:

Why did I long to be below? I don't know. I just remember that I did and that this descent seemed a difficult but necessary step up life's ladder. The whole Alaskan experience was a sub-conscious attempt to escape from the world, to put off what-ever was in store for me; the farther down inside a ship I went, the better the hiding place. Moreover, I wanted to test myself—

throw myself into any flame that was handy, to see if I could stand the heat. (*The Points of My Compass*, 225)

Perhaps this experience was the challenge that White had been thinking about since those days in 1917 when he had felt uneasy about not being in the war, which had been the test of many men of a slightly earlier generation. White's was a healthier experience than war and, though shorter, must have been in its way almost as intense. But unlike war, it left White no bitterness, no disillusionment; rather, it gave him a new sharp sense of the reality of men, of the vividness of life. At the end of "The Years of Wonder," White describes a storm at sea, a storm that was an epiphany of the whole experience. It may be meaningful that in his description he uses the word "battle":

In the fury of the storm, thought was impossible; the future was expunged by wind and water; I lived at last in the present, and the present was magnificent—rich and beautiful and awesome. It gave me all the things I wanted from life, and it was as though I drank each towering wave as it came aboard, as though I would ever after be athirst. At last I had adjusted, temporarily, to a difficult world and had conquered it; others were sick, I bloomed with health. In the noise of battle, all the sad silences of my brooding and foreboding were lost. I had always feared and loved the sea, and this gale was my bride and we had a three-day honeymoon, a violent, tumultuous time of undreamed-of ecstasy and satisfaction. (*The Points of My Compass*, 239—40)

I have quoted extensively from "The Years of Wonder" because it both describes a critical period of White's life and represents the best of his writing. But we must be wary about biographical generalizations. To a query of mine, White wrote: "As for 'The Years of Wonder' being a kind of baptism, I was being baptized regularly every hour on the hour for about ten years of general uncertainty and insolvency of mind and pocket. I don't think Alaska should shoulder the whole burden of this dunking."[27]

After Alaska, White returned to New York; for a while he was unemployed and as he said, he was "a happy man

. . . for I had no job and no mosquito bites."[28] Even jobless,
White found sustenance and satisfaction in New York;
he was referring to this period when he wrote, "I spent a
solid year once experimenting with idleness and finding
out exactly what it was like to occupy myself with nothing at all over a wide range of country."[29] White, who
lived with three other Cornellians at 112 West 13th Street,
wasn't, of course, doing "nothing." He contributed to
"The Conning Tower," he had a canoe and a catboat,
he saw on occasion a pretty face that captivated him; and,
above all, he came to know New York and to find there
not only privacy and loneliness—"the terrible loneliness
of midmorning" (*The Second Tree from the Corner*, 216)—
but also a stimulus to creativity, and the time to write,
time to think. In a sketch that he wrote, a character who
seems to represent him mused that in New York "was un-
questionably the closest written page in the book of his
life" (213).

But the occasional poem, the long times to think, to
walk, could not sustain White indefinitely; still looking
for the right job, he tried advertising, working first for
the Frank Seaman agency then for J. H. Newmark. The
advertising business required as many compromises
from the creative artist then as today. What J. Thorne
Smith wrote in 1922 certainly held for advertising when
White started working in 1924: "Generally speaking . . .
advertising is the graveyard of literary aspiration in which
the spirits of the defeated aspirants, wielding a momentary
power over a public that rejected their efforts, blackjack
it into buying the most amazing assortment of purely use-
less and cheaply manufactured commodities that has ever
marked the decline of culture and common sense. These
men are either caught early after their flight from college,
or else recruited from the newspaper world."[30] As we
shall see, White would not agree entirely with this statement, although Smith has stated well the predicament of
the creative artist.

Mostly, White's job was that of production, "handling
electrotypes and stuff like that and occasionally writing
a little copy."[31] He had no liking for the work; but, as

he told Susan Frank, "I had to earn my living." He didn't like the complexity of the advertising business, and he could see, perhaps was afraid of, the lure that advertising held: the ad man, White noted, "believes himself to be creating literature"; and because he likes to see his stuff in print, he works hard.[32]

According to Ingersoll, White wrote some material for a mail-order course in automobile salesmanship; when an order for the course came in from a barber in Wisconsin, White "resigned, full of remorse" (*"The New Yorker,"* 86). The resignation may not have been so precipitous as Ingersoll states; White was probably writing about himself when, in a "Notes and Comment" item for June 1, 1929, he describes a young man as follows: "[He] had come to New York and taken a job in an advertising agency writing mail-order copy. The fierce transition from Shelley and Keats to blurbs incorporating all known principles of attention-getting, appetite-appeal, and anti-sales-resistance saddened the young man and he went into a decline and finally resigned." The young man, White continues, later went to the Public Library with a pair of scissors and quietly snipped out the ads he had written from the magazines in which they had appeared.

In retrospect, White's view of advertising was surprisingly moderate. "Actually," he wrote some years later, "I believed that the world of advertising was essentially a good thing, and I still believe that."[33] But he did feel that writing advertisements was not a job for creative people. Still the advertising experience had been important to White; it was an essential part of his continuing self-discovery, his self-testing. He wrote Thurber that he had hung on to advertising because he had no confidence in his ability in the world of letters.[34]

It was *The New Yorker* that saved White: "I managed to squeak out of that [advertising] when *The New Yorker* was founded in 1925."[35] White simply could not do his best under the tension of a newspaper, or in the daily routine of an office. "The weekly magazine," he said, "gave me my chance . . . because it was a different kind of pressure . . . . It was a much more flexible thing than a daily newspaper."[36] White didn't leave the advertising world completely, though; for a year or so, advertising and his work for *The New Yorker* overlapped; as late as 1926, he wrote some advertising for the Cunard Line. *The New Yorker* was precisely the place for a man whose personal "giants" were Don Marquis, Heywood Broun, Christopher Morley, Franklin P. Adams, Robert Benchley, Frank Sullivan, Dorothy Parker, Alexander Woollcott, Ring Lardner, and Stephen Vincent Benet,[37] and whose congenial form was the editorial. And a new magazine was a good place for a writer waiting to show what he could do.

White's first piece, "Defense of the Bronx River," appeared in *The New Yorker* on May 9, 1925; later in the year, other pieces and some poems were accepted; after writing an account of buttermilk being spilled on him by a waitress, he made the important discovery "that the world would pay a man for setting down a simple, legible account of his own misfortunes" (*The Second Tree from the Corner*, 214). By 1926, White was working part-time for *The New Yorker*, writing tag-lines for the newsbreaks department. Also that year, he went to England and the Continent on a trip paid for by Cunard in return for his writing the script for a promotional film advertising their College Cabin Class. By 1927, White was working full-time for *The New Yorker* and writing a fair portion of the "Notes and Comment" department. He still had other occupations, however, and in 1928 and 1929 took part in operating Camp Otter, a boy's camp in Ontario, of which he was part owner.

The years of wonder were by no means over, but White was beginning to find what he could do well and was doing it. I say "beginning," because there was still a lot of uncertainty and unrest in White during those early *New Yorker* days, at least until 1929—a loneliness and a poignancy that is movingly expressed in a sketch written in 1927, "An Evening on Ice." Finding himself in Madison Square Garden, skates under arm, and no ice, White stands, a simple figure defeated by a complex world, in front of a booth where a girl is demonstrating silver polish: "My years hung heavy round my head; my mawkishness, my irresponsible way of living bore me down, and I saw that all my futilities, all my willingness to go alone in the world, making small progress, had led at last to the woebegone spectacle of a dismal man, standing, ice-skates under his arm, in front of a silver polish booth!" (*Quo Vadimus*, 186)

For White, 1929 was an epochal year, but it wasn't the stock-market crash that was significant. He published two books that year—*The Lady Is Cold*, and *Is Sex Necessary?* (James Thurber was co-author of the latter)—and, "the most dramatic episode in his career,"[38] he married Katharine S. Angell. Some, perhaps most, of his uncertainty and "insolvency of mind and pocket" was gone.

CHAPTER 2

# "Words But Catch the Moment's Tint"

WHITE'S first published work (*c.* 1910) was a poem and it may be that Morris Bishop is right in his feeling that the center of White's interest was poetry.[1] Still, poetry was clearly not White's only early literary interest: his contributions to the Manuscript Club included prose as well as poetry, and of course most of his work on the *Sun* involved prose. Nonetheless, White's first book, *The Lady Is Cold,* was a collection of his poems written in the years up to 1929, and White was to write later: "I am jealous of them [poets]. I would rather be one than anything."[2] His second volume of poetry, *The Fox of Peapack and Other Poems,* appeared in 1938. White has published some poetry since, and not all of his poems written up to 1938 had been included in the two volumes. In the discussion that follows, however, we are concerned with the poetry in those two collections. In Chapter VII we consider some of the other poems.

Although most of White's poetry is light verse, his best poems are not always his humorous poems, and his humorous ones often have an ironic twist or comment that gives them a serious tone. Those poems where humor is the chief or sole effect are apt to be too topical or too insubstantial to be effective; some, however, are successful. "Algernon Charles Swinburne, Slightly Cock-Eyed, Sees the Old Year Out," a skillful parody of "The Garden of Proserpine," will appeal to those readers who know Swinburne and remember the 1920's.

We find reminders of other poets, too, in *The Lady Is Cold*: Walt Whitman, Vachel Lindsay, William Wordsworth. But White is best in this collection in his lyrical poems, especially those about nature and the pathos of man's spirit confined by the drudging complexity of the city. The title poem, "The Lady Is Cold," describes a man sitting by a cold statue in winter and seeing hopeful signs of spring. The poem ends:

> The earth is but held in solution,
>     And March will release before long
> The lady in brazen ablution,
>     The trees and the fountain in song!

The clear and simple language conveys nicely a sense of sparseness; at the same time, the rising anapestic rhythm gives the poem an anticipatory effect consonant with the meaning.

Effective also is the relatively early poem "Subway People," first published in *The New Yorker* (December 5, 1925). With a rhythm strongly suggestive of Vachel Lindsay and Stephen Vincent Benet, White captures in this poem something of the aimlessness of life, and something of its pathos:

> Sitters, waiters,—riders to eternity,
> Shuffling in the shadow world, all day long;
> Standers, thinkers,—joggers to eternity,
> Swaying to the rhythm of the sad loud song.

Linked with this poem in subject matter, another, "Commuter," has a curious history. According to White, he and Howard Cushman "entertained for a short spell the insane notion that we might write a dictionary of the English language in quatrains." "Commuter" was to be one of the poems for the letter *C*.[3]

By and large, we cannot claim a great deal for the poems in this first volume; White is too restrained, and at times there is too much distance between the poet and the scene he describes; in most of these poems, he comments

quietly on the daily routine of city life, its minor conflicts, its tensions. He describes late evening and early
morning rambles, the chance appearance of a pretty face,
and the brief contact with people that brings a transient
sense of unity; taking a half-whimsical look at himself,
he celebrates his minor victories, and is amused by his
weaknesses.

A modest quality, as well as restraint, exists in many of
these poems, almost as if White were afraid of being too
serious, too involved—or perhaps too conscious of the
danger of destroying his sensitive perception of life by
putting it into words:

> Words but catch the moment's tint,
> Though their meaning rock you;
> Never one shall fly to print
> Will not live to mock you.

White experimented with a wide variety of poetic forms
in *The Lady Is Cold*, but a kind of caution also appears;
he is ultimately conventional. The poetic echoes we find
are of the Romantics, or of Carl Sandburg, Vachel Lindsay,
Archibald MacLeish, not of Ezra Pound, W. B. Yeats, or
T. S. Eliot. In an occasional line we see the  promise of the
better poetry of White's *The Fox of Peapack*—the sharper
images, the stronger statements. In a pleasant but minor
effort about a morning-glory vine, "Window Box," we
suddenly read: "And insects gnawed the stem at night,/
And Death hung bat-like from the eaves." Perhaps the
best lines of the whole volume are in "The Spirit of St.
Christopher," a well-constructed sonnet about Lindbergh's
inability to resist flying during a beautiful night: "What
are they like, those stretches of blue moor,/ The lovely
fields of freedom, sown with light?"

Thematically, the poems of *The Lady Is Cold* express
many of White's basic ideas and views: his love of New
York; his sharp awareness of the price one pays for living
in the city; his nostalgic love of simplicity; his admiration for the stubborn endurance of natural life and beauty
in an urban setting; his passion for freedom, coupled

with his need for love and responsibility; his sense of the transiency of life; and his half-serious, ever-present fear of death.

Some of the poems of *The Fox of Peapack* had been published before 1929, but the majority appeared in the early 1930's; there were at least five events, forces, that had a strong impact on White after *The Lady Is Cold*: his marriage to Katharine S. Angell in 1929, the birth of his son Joel in 1930, the Depression, the New Deal, and the rising totalitarianism in Europe. These events gave to the poems in *The Fox of Peapack* a seriousness and maturity that had been missing in the earlier collection; as David McCord said in a review, White "has come a long way since his earlier collection."[4] But the book contains, as well as serious poems, some of White's best humorous poetry.

One difference between the poems in this collection and those in the earlier one is that many in this begin with a newspaper comment and develop from it. This approach may tend to produce limited and topical poems but it also suggests that White was moving closer to his material. *The Fox of Peapack* has fewer lyrical poems, fewer bits of whimsy; it has, on the other hand, stronger and more vigorous statements. Although we find, for example, references to advertising in *The Lady Is Cold*, they are light, scarcely critical; in "The Silence of the Gears" from *The Fox of Peapack* we discover a White who speaks of the "whoring Voices of the reasonable air/ In fifteen-minute lozenges of pleasure."

Marriage and a son gave White fresh themes; in "Complicated Thoughts about a Small Son," he sees a new purpose in his life:

> And since, to write in blood and breath
> Was fairer than my fairest dream,
> The manuscript I leave for death
> Is you, whose life supplied its theme.

In "Song for the Delegates," addressed to the Geneva Disarmament Conference, 1932, he thinks of his son in another way:

> The prospects still are extra fine
> That in no mimic battle line
> Your son, O delegate, and mine
> Will die by getting blown apart.

Some of these poems are effective; but, of course, some have suffered from time. Parodies of Gertrude Stein seem less relevant now than they did in the 1930's when her reputation was higher; a poem about Boake Carter, no matter how good, means little to one who does not remember that "baleful voice" and Philco's inclined sounding board. But not all poems about specific incidents fade. Among White's best serious poems are "Flying over Ethiopian Mountain Ranges," "Hymn to the Dark," and "I Paint What I See."

In the first of these White responds to the notorious comment by Vittorio Mussolini about bombing in Ethiopia: "I remember," said Mussolini, "that one group of horsemen gave me the impression of a budding rose as the bombs fell in their midst. It was exceptionally good fun." The comment was shocking then; we hope it is still, though Mussolini's words may seem merely honest and naïve to a world grown accustomed to "clean bomb," "low yield," and the American pilot's reference to a "Kentucky Turkey shoot" in Viet Nam.

White, at any rate, seeing in the comment an attitude that violated all decent respect for life, responds with strong feeling. The comment provides White with a central and ironic image, the rose:

> Where horsemen's blood runs sickly
>     To the absorbent earth,
> The rose, unfolding quickly
>     To give the canker birth,
> Reveals a wormlike beauty
>     To the new ranks of youth,
> Their hands upraised in duty,
>     Their heels unshod with ruth.

In an earlier poem, "Harvest of Half-Truths" (1931), White had asked, half-seriously, "How can Man (half monkey) issue/ From the half-depths to the deep?" What was said lightly then becomes serious and ironic in the present poem: "And Man, once called *Erectus*,/ Will crawl once more, and bleed." The poem ends with a return to the opening image:

> The Ethiopian horsemen
>   Once more in light must die
> To make the rose of beauty
>   For young men in the sky.
>
> Then earth from night shall borrow,
>   And the strange chapter close,
> Where diggers of tomorrow
>   Scratch at the fossil rose.

This poem reveals some of White's weaknesses as well as his strengths. It is not an involved statement, there are no complexities, no metrical subtleties, and there are some awkward lines: "They sit, and drop the little/ Bright shaft with death endowed." But White was not writing for an academic audience, for critics trained in explication and analysis, but for a broadly and probably vaguely educated audience, many of whom might well have turned away from the difficulties of reading some modern poets. A case can be made for simplicity and for a clearly expressed moral purpose, and these White has.

"Hymn to the Dark" (1935), written in free verse somewhat suggestive of MacLeish, and one of White's most serious poems, indicts the forces pushing man towards war; in terms of imagery, it is his most sophisticated poem. Men stand now, writes White, on the threshold of a new Dark Ages, the "blinding dusk of the world":

> Like children, hand in hand,
> Our eyeballs blistered with unbearable brightness,
> The neon hemorrhaging, trickling from the tubes,
> Spilled on the earth like blood from a serpent,
> The earth absorbent, the dusk tangible,
> Culture, with one thread loose, at last unwinding.

The poem was published shortly after the Italian invasion of Ethiopia, and White speaks of totalitarianism and
of the youths

> who follow Hate
Shaped like a swastika, sadist economies,
the dominance of steel and the sword stainless,
The dissenting tongues cleft at the root and bleeding,
Singers with their throats cut, trying
(While yet there's time) to point out where the venom is . . . .

The poem concludes with a despairing prayer:

> This is the light that failed. Oh Christ,
Make us an end of light if this be light,
Make us an end of sound if this ethereal
Babble, caught in the glowing tubes, translated into waves,
Be sound. If darkness comes, let the dark be
Velvet and cool . . . kind to the eyes, to the hands
Opened to the dust, and to the heart pressed
To the rediscovered earth, the heart reclaimed
For the millionth time by the slow sanity
Of the recurring tides.

The appeal to the earth as the only hope typifies White's
faith in the virtue of natural simplicity, in the soil, in the
recurring processes of nature—the faith he hinted at in
*The Lady Is Cold*; the faith that became more than words
when, in 1938, White left New York for his farm in Maine.
This poem is his most emotional response to violence,
to Fascism and Nazism; characteristically, he responds
in terms of human suffering, not political systems; in
terms of the healing, renewing quality of nature, not political reform.

One of White's best known poems, "I Paint What I See,"
concerns the controversy over the Rivera murals in Rockefeller Center. The poem, a good example of White's
use of current events as literary material, began in part,
at least, with an article in *The New York Times* of May
10, 1933, where Rivera had been quoted as saying: "The
religious are attacking me because I am religious. I paint

what I see." The *Times* then reports that Nelson Rockefeller had asked Rivera about the colors he had used, and had suggested that they were too bright for the Rockefeller taste. In the poem, Rockefeller's question becomes: " 'Do you use any red in the beard of a saint?/ 'If you do, is it terribly red, or faint?/ 'Do you use any blue? Is it Prussian?' "

The heart of the controversy was not color, however, but the portrait of Lenin in the mural. Rivera offered to put in the head of Lincoln, or McCormick, though he was not willing to remove Lenin; White plays upon this nicely:

> 'I'll take out a couple of people drinkin'
> 'And put in a picture of Abraham Lincoln;
> 'I could even give you McCormick's reaper
> 'And still not make my art much cheaper
> 'But the head of Lenin has got to stay
> 'Or my friends will give me the bird today,
> 'The bird, the bird, forever.'

Another point Rockefeller had made, according to the *Times*, was that Rockefeller Center was not a private house, but a public building; in the poem, his objection becomes: " 'For this, as you know, is a public hall,/ 'And people want doves, or a tree in fall.' " The end of the poem may have been overly optimistic; when Rockefeller says, "And after all,/ It's *my* wall," the last line has "We'll see if it is,' said Rivera." White probably wrote the poem after the first news reports, for later, of course, Rivera lost his fight: it *was* Rockefeller's wall.

The poem is one of White's happiest combinations of wit and seriousness. His refusal to take Rivera too seriously, to take too doctrinaire a position on the matter ("Or my friends will give me the bird today") may seem to some a lack of commitment; but, by avoiding the role of either professional liberal or conservative, White in the long run may have spoken with his most effective voice.

Comparison with MacLeish's "Frescoes for Mr. Rockefeller's City" is inevitable. There can be no denial that MacLeish's poem is more elaborate, more involved tech-

nically, and more eloquent. Interestingly, though, Mac-
Leish, like White, can make fun of the radical, while being
critical of the establishment. Few critics would hesitate in
judging MacLeish's poem to be better, but the poems are
not entirely comparable. White's is immediate; it demands,
for complete comprehension and appreciation, a recent
reading of the report in the *Times*; and it has throughout
a light-hearted tone. As a more temperate statement, White's
poem may indeed have gained as much sympathy for Rivera's
position as MacLeish's.

In "Notes and Comment" for June 24, 1933, White adds
a footnote to his poem. He strolled, he says, through Rockefeller Plaza one day and gazed "with reverent amuse-
ment at the gray canvas that conceals the work of Señor
Rivera. In some far away century that mural may turn up
again; it will be discovered, probably, by a dinosaur looking for a good place to lay some eggs" *(Every Day Is Saturday,* 182).

Reviewers of White's two volumes of poetry have praised
his work. They have in general, however, considered him
as a versifier, rather than as a poet. David McCord was
the exception when, comparing White with Ogden Nash,
he wrote of *The Fox of Peapack*: "His light verse (and a
few serious poems in this ample book) have a quality of
wistfulness and true poetry that Nash has never shown."[5]
The problem is that if we consider White merely a writer
of humorous verse, he can be praised—and probably
ignored. If he is to be taken more seriously, certain difficulties arise. He has not developed a distinctive poetic
style of his own, yet on the other hand he does not seem
clearly to belong to any of the more vigorous streams of
modern poetry. He does not emerge from William Blake or
Walt Whitman, or from the Metaphysical poets; he is not,
as we have noted, a follower of W. B. Yeats, Ezra Pound
or T. S. Eliot; he has not evolved the colloquial style or
broad appeal of a Robert Frost; and except for a few lines
here and there, he has nothing of the musical images
of a Dylan Thomas. Leonard Bacon is at least partly right
when he says of White that "in general there is a certain

lack of ease about his verse. It hasn't the motion and grace
of his prose."[6] Bacon isn't entirely right, but the comment
does lead to a general truth: that White's great strength
*is* his prose, not his poetry.

So far as I know, the best case that can be made for
White's poetry has been made by Morris Bishop in his
introduction to *One Man's Meat*. Speaking of the poems
in White's two collections, Bishop notes that many of them
are "mere trifles, amusing developments of small observations" (vii). However, Bishop continues, the best of
White's poems should interest the critic: "For E. B. White
and a few others are creating a new mid-form between
Light Verse and Heavy Verse, between the determined
comic conviction of the one and the pretentious obscurity
of the other" (vii). These poets, says Bishop, "aim at lucid-
ity, at the communication of their meaning to the large
number of people who are responsive to poetic form and
feeling but who are rebuffed by the hermetics of our time"
(viii).

The "heavy poets" of today, Bishop adds, have alien-
ated the traditional audience of the poet—"the college
type of man or woman who reads seriously and with the
expectation of finding in books some recognition of his
own experience. Most heavy poets now despise this class
of reader" (viii). Bishop makes his point vigorously, and
he takes a kind of pleasure in his speculation about the
future of poetry: "It would be amusing," he says, "if the
thin stream of Modern Poetry should run out and lose itself
in the sands of unintelligibility, and if the mid-form of
E. B. White and his compeers should become the source
for the poetry of the future" (viii).

If there is a "mid-form"—and I share Bishop's hope
that there is—it would seem to be more likely in Frost
than in White. In truth, White's poetry cannot be seen
aside from White. If his real significance lies in his point of
view, in what he represents as a spokesman for "the true
aristocracy of mind and spirit," then the ultimate significance of his poetry lies in how it helps to define what he
represents. Since his prose defines that position far better

than his poetry, his poetry must take a secondary role in any final assessment.

If some of White's poetry can be read today with pleasure, and if some of it deserves more critical attention than it has received, still, no poem of White's can rate with the best of Eliot, Auden, or Thomas, and surely we cannot call those poets part of a "thin stream," or workers in the "sands of unintelligibility." White has been the great spokesman for what might be considered a mid-form, but a mid-form of ideas, of human warmth—the viewing of life not with cosmic seriousness but with tolerant affection. White speaks for this mid-form, not the mid-form of poetry.

## CHAPTER 3

# White, *The New Yorker*, and the Growth of a Moralist

## I *Humor*

FROM 1927, when White began working full time for *The New Yorker*, until 1938, when he left New York to live in Maine, he spent a substantial part of his time writing part or all of the "Notes and Comment" department of *The New Yorker*, writing the tag-lines for newsbreaks, and serving as one of the editors of *The New Yorker*. In addition, as we have seen, he published two volumes of poetry. He also, with James Thurber, wrote *Is Sex Necessary?* (1929); and he wrote numerous sketches, articles, and stories, most of which were published in *The New Yorker*, and some reprinted in *Quo Vadimus?* (1939). In short, almost everything White wrote from 1927 to 1938 had some connection with *The New Yorker* and showed the spirit and attitude that he brought with him to the magazine, or developed while he was working for it.

The story of *The New Yorker* has been told in two books, Thurber's *The Years with Ross* and Kramer's *Ross and The New Yorker*, as well as in a number of articles. Some more specific mention needs to be made, however, of White's part in *The New Yorker*; for his success is connected with that magazine, just as its success is connected with him. White's importance on *The New Yorker* has been noted by a large number of writers: Russell Maloney, for example, asserted that, next to Ross, "Thurber and White have most deeply impressed their personalities on the magazine."[1] Others have singled out White, Thurber, Wolcott Gibbs, and Katharine White as the major figures on *The New Yorker*. More specific was Stanley E. Hyman's observation that the heart of *The New Yorker* was "The Talk of the Town," and *its* heart, "Notes and Comment."[2] *The New Yorker*, according to Ralph Ingersoll, considered "Notes and Comment" the "spearhead of its purpose . . . . It would not be unfair to say that if Ross created the body, Thurber and White are the soul of *The New Yorker*."[3] To Morris Bishop, White made "Notes and Comment" "something memorable in modern journalism. . . . The 'Notes and Comment' page made of *The New Yorker* a personality, a soul."[4]

There is, of course, more to *The New Yorker* than "Notes and Comment." Still, for many readers it has been one of the most appealing parts of the magazine. Only a small fraction of White's contributions to "Notes and Comment" have been reprinted. A selection of the best of them from 1928 to 1934 is in *Every Day Is Saturday* (1934); many of those from 1943 to 1946 about world government are in *The Wild Flag*. With the exception of an item or two in 1926, White's contributions began in 1927, when he wrote over two hundred items, many times doing the whole page himself.

Most of these early comments are of little interest today; they are incisive, witty observations, often on trivial matters: the problem of cashing a ten-dollar bill at Woolworth's, references to jokes and scandals in New York, comments on items in newspapers, and occasionally a little gem. If they are not particularly significant, there was no intention that they should be. But they are well-written, and they point forward to what White becomes: the spokesman for freedom and privacy; the moralist in the best sense of the word.

However, it was *Is Sex Necessary?*, not "Notes and Comment," that first made White's name well-known. The first book he published after *The Lady Is Cold*, White's contribution (James Thurber wrote about half the book) was the "Foreword," Chapters 2, 4, 6, 8, and "Answers to

Hard Questions." The book was very much a part of the 1920's, and very much a part of White's early *New Yorker* days. In fact, we might say that the book, light-hearted spoof that it is, represents the maturity of White's first period of intellectual growth—if that is not too pretentious a way of talking about him. It is a humorous book, yet beneath its humor it makes a serious point, more serious than almost anything that White had said in *The New Yorker* up to that time. The subject of sex was overburdened with glib books that pretended to speak with authority and with better books that *did* speak with authority. But, as White said, paraphrasing Wolcott Gibbs, "the heavy writers had got sex down and were breaking its arm."[5]

Commentators on the era have noted the number of writers on the subject of marriage and sex: Ellen Key, Edward Carpenter, Havelock Ellis, Bertrand Russell, for example, were all popular during the 1920's. Frederick J. Hoffman notes that "an insatiable curiosity about sex was one of the most obvious characteristics of these years. Frankness about sexual matters, together with an avid reading of books dealing with problems of sex, gave the subject an exaggerated importance."[6] In 1920, he adds, "there were hundreds of popular summaries, expositions, and distortions of Freud's original works, together with a growing number of works allegedly presenting the psychologies of Jung, Adler and other psychoanalysts."[7]

There was plenty of room for satire. Joseph Collins, in *The Doctor Looks at Love and Life* (1926), has this silly distortion of Freud: Dr. Johnson had answered Boswell's question about what he would do with a newborn child with the simple reply, "Feed it." Were Dr. Johnson alive today, says Collins, "and convinced that the teaching of Freud were found in fact, it is likely that he would say, 'I should kill it' " (237). The last part of James Oppenheim's *Behind Your Front* (1928) includes an apparently serious analysis, complete with diagrams, of the relation between nose shapes and introverted and extroverted personality types.

White began taking a humorous interest in the subject
of sex well before 1929, for he writes in "Notes and Comment" for May 14, 1927, that

our notion is that sex, because of American naïveté, has fallen
into various categories, most of which have been too pompous.
Its biological, sociological, and psychoanalytical aspects have
been fully plumbed, almost to the point of our losing interest.
Therefore it was a relief to find a wholesome bookseller—well
below Fourteenth Street—who had thrown the whole matter back
to its merry origins: in a window devoted to question books,
games, and other books on entertainment, the wag had placed a
volume entitled 'Plain Facts of Sex.'

On July 2, 1927, White comments that "sex is troubling
Bishop Manning, as it is everybody who has any time at
all to give to it." And on March 23, 1929, he observes
that "sex is now so academic it's no fun any more. Kiss
a girl and it reminds you of a footnote." Anyway, by 1929
both White and Thurber were troubled enough to take
the time to rescue sex from the pompous psychological
and sociological jargon to which it was falling victim.
    The approach of *Is Sex Necessary?* is simple enough:
both authors parody the serious writers on the subject.
They make light of complexities, they take a mock-serious
attitude toward the obvious, they delight in reducing the
case-history technique to an absurdity, and they make fun
of those writers who proceeded by definitions. Thurber's
inimitable drawings, often skillful parodies of the sober
illustrations in some of the books on sex, would almost
have made the book a success by themselves.
    From the title on, the satire never lags. In Chapter II,
"How to Tell Love from Passion," White cuts through the
pages of arduous and tormented jargon of other writers:
"When I say love in this article, you will take it to mean
*the pleasant confusion which we know exists.* When I
say passion, I *mean* passion." In his next chapter, White
surprises his readers by observing that "The Sexual Revolution" was not a new freedom and promiscuity in young
girls coming to New York but an affliction of "schmalhausen
trouble" (caused by small apartments). The young girls end

up "giving sex the air." There are similar surprises in White's other two chapters: the real problems, we discover, are frigidity in men, and the difficulties children have in telling their parents the facts of life.

Though White has modestly stated in his introduction that Thurber's opening chapter, "The Nature of the American Male; a Study of Pedestalism," is the best in the book, we need not agree. The chapters are on the whole remarkably even, stylistically and in content, with White's chapter, "How to Tell Love from Passion," as good as any in the book. The continuing popularity of the book is evidence that White might have been wrong when he asserted that "passion, to the modern, is not much more mysterious or baffling than a sneeze or a yawn" (Introduction, xv). We still need to see the funny side of sex, as Malcolm Muggeridge, Terry Southern, Vladimir Nabokov, and Kingsley Amis, among others, remind us.

The book is not faultless: some of the humorous gags of the 1920's have paled, and the funny footnote seems less funny now, but there is not too much of that sort of thing and taken all in all, the book represents the best of White's light, humorous satire. It is carefree, untouched by the deeper concerns of the 1920's expressed by Scott Fitzgerald, William Faulkner, Ernest Hemingway. If White and Thurber have not written a profound book, they have written with assurance. White's share of the book, more successful as humor than his poetry up to 1929, is written with more confidence, and is less topical. We sometimes feel with White's poetry that he would really prefer to be serious; there is none of that feeling with regard to *Is Sex Necessary?*, a *tour de force* that continues to amuse with its playful wit.

White, then, began as a poet and as a humorist, and it was as a humorist that he first attracted much attention. Although he never lost his humorous touch, a retrospective view of White suggests that humor is not his enduring quality. Serious themes emerge, and humor becomes more and more a means to an end, not an end in itself. Still, at this point in White's career, it is his humor that we remember.

White's earlier work—pieces written, say, from 1928 to 1931—contain much of the characteristic wit of the day: the use of " 'em," or, "Oh, is that so?"; or this sort of thing: "Means cutting the jawbone. Yes, sir, the old jawbone." Or again, " 'I am Mr. Aiken,' he said . . . That was how I knew he was Mr. Aiken." And finally, the joke about pronunciation: "a little Irish girl named McGheogheoghan (pronounced McVeigh)." As White developed as a writer, this rhetorical funny business disappeared, and something better began to appear—like his parody of Hemingway in *The Second Tree from the Corner*.

One of the first jobs White had on *The New Yorker* (he still does it) was to write the tag-lines for the newsbreaks department. Here he has been consistently and brilliantly witty, and it is hard to see how anyone else could do as well. Many of these tag-lines have been reprinted in two collections: *Ho-Hum* (1931), and *Another Ho-Hum* (1932). The tag-line is a curiously specialized art, and whatever gifts are necessary, White has them. He avoids the obvious gags; and by a witty irrelevance, or an ironic jab, he elevates the silly misprint, the odd comment, or the pretentious, badly written news item into something better than it deserves to be. He delights, too, in pouncing on the ambiguities in slipshod English. It was a talent White had employed a few times while working on *The Cornell Daily Sun* and had developed farther while he was on *The Seattle Times*. Here is an example from White's early *New Yorker* days (the last line is White's comment):

LOST—Male fox hound, brown head, yellow legs, blue body with large black spots on left side, male. Also female, white with red head and spot on hip.—*Fayette (Mo.) Democrat Leader.*

Those aren't dogs, those are nasturtiums. (*Ho-Hum,* 60)

## II  *More Serious Matters*

Before the stock market crash of 1929, White appeared to accept without much thought the economic prosperity of the country. "To date," he writes in 1928, "New York has shown nothing but progress. Hopefully we wait the first signs of decadence." But, he concludes, "business goes on right through the top of the day, prosperity mounting over a clank of coffee cups" (*Every Day Is Saturday*, 13). Of course White had been serious before the Depression, as some of the poems in *The Lady Is Cold* clearly enough show. Yet, in his prose especially, White could view the life around him in the late 1920's and the early days of the Depression with a pleasant equanimity and could comment on its foibles with a smile.

Secure himself, both financially and, through his marriage, emotionally, he could afford to be critical and yet objective about life. At first, he was not disturbed by the stock-market decline; like many people in the late fall of 1929, he had no suspicion of what was coming; and, again like many, he appeared to expect the early return of prosperity. Although on November 2, 1929, he writes a comment on fear—"Fear, running through the jungle like flame, strong as ever"—he can also speak of the market break as the Wall Street "interlude" (December 28, 1929). As late as 1931, he speaks of those people and corporations who were quite prosperous and didn't know what to do with their money as the "most amusing spectacle of the slump" (November 7, 1931).[8]

By 1932, however, White viewed the Depression with more serious understanding. Henry Ford had said something about the "normal processes of industry and business," and White asks: "How do we know that two-million-men-idle isn't normal under our system of government by investigation, peace by appropriation, and happiness by aërial dissemination of dance music?" (*Every Day Is Saturday*, 115). White knew what joblessness could do to a man's spirit. His own unemployment in the early 1920's had been unrelated to the national economy, and he had not experienced abject proverty, but he writes with feeling about the problem: "Being out of a job perforates the walls of the mind, and thoughts seep off into strange channels" (143). Even the bonus marchers of 1932, for whose cause White had little sympathy, were symptom-

atic of the price the Depression was exacting: "That
army was something more than just a lobby: it was the
expression of men's desire to huddle together when their
courage is gone" (143).

White was pleased that one of his ideas about unemployment was apparently taken up by the government:
in July, 1932, he had suggested that an army be established "to give men a change of scene and a change of
heart; an army in which men could enlist for a short term,
not to destroy the enemy, but to recapture their own soul"
(143). On October 7, 1933, he speaks approvingly of the
newly established CCC (Civilian Conservation Corps); and
he reminds his readers that he had suggested something
like it a year or so ago. White didn't seriously suppose that
he had played a part in starting the CCC. His comments
do show, however, that he had been thinking realistically
in terms of social change.

Still, the effect of the Depression on White was general
rather than specific. He did not become an economic
theorist, a technocrat, or a revolutionary, and he wrote
rather infrequently on the Depression. His most sustained
comment, a little pamphlet, *Alice Through the Cellophane*
(1933), is a generally lighthearted discussion (which White
does not now regard very highly) that makes some serious
points about the American economic system. White argues
that our economy has too much momentum and is too
complex: the time has come to simplify, to "produce goods
only in amounts that people need instead of what promo-
tion experts say people can absorb or what advertising
geniuses think they can chivvy the world into buying" (22).

Although White did not become a Communist or start
producing proletarian novels, his writing, after the Depression seemed permanent, did attain a seriousness
that had only been hinted at before. It was not precisely
a "time of regeneration"[9] for White, but he did think more
deeply about politics, religion, progress, the unrest in
Europe, social and economic problems, and particularly
about the increasing complexity of American society.

It is customary to explain White's attitude toward simplicity and complexity in terms of Thoreau, whose writ-

ing without doubt had strong influence on him. "Whenever he went anywhere," wrote Dale Kramer, "he packed his *Walden* as naturally as his toothbrush" *(Ross and The New Yorker*, 141). But Thoreau's influence was, perhaps, as much stylistic as thematic. Although White may have studied Thoreau in college (in his senior year he took a survey course in American literature), it was not until 1927 that he mentions buying a copy of *Walden (Second Tree from the Corner*, 94). He refers to Thoreau many times, from his early work to his latest collection, *Points of My Compass*, in which his tribute to Thoreau is a summary statement of his feelings.

Even as a boy, however, White seemed to have been thinking of the simple life. In "Stratagem for Retirement," he says that "I find that I still hold to the same opinions that were mine when I was thirteen. I think a man should learn to swim in the pool of time, should tuck up his affairs so they fit into a canoe, and having snugged all down, should find out what bird is his eagle, and climb the tree" (87). As is often the case in matters of "influence," White was probably drawn to Thoreau because he gave eloquent confirmation to attitudes White already had. Thurber, for example, mentioning the spirit of Thoreau in White, notes also that two of White's favorite books were Bruun's *Van Zanten's Happy Days*, and Alain-Fournier's *The Wanderer (Le Grand Meaulnes)*.[10] The former, with its idyllic and touching picture of the simple life in the South Sea Islands, was another confirmation of pre-existing attitudes. However, there is more to say about Thoreau and White, and we return to this topic in Chapter VIII.

In his early comments in *Every Day Is Saturday*, White remarks playfully about the complex life: when a hundred clerks in an insurance office moved from one building to another, he asks incredulously, "And didn't any of the clerks escape?" (13). He regrets the loss in men of "the sufficiency of being animal" (58); he says that the healthiest countries in the world are "those in which men did the most tangible tasks" (146). In a more biting remark, he challenges Edward A. Filene's theory that we all want the same thing—some way of having more people buy more things. White reminds Filene that Thoreau, commenting on superfluous possessions, had mentioned seeing a dried tapeworm among the life-time accumulations of a deacon.

In *Quo Vadimus* (1939) White speaks with a clearer and sometimes more trenchant voice about complexity. Some of the sketches here, from the late 1920's and early 1930's, represent the same playful attitude White had shown in *Every Day Is Saturday*. A later sketch, however, "The Family Which Dwelt Apart," though fanciful and humorous in part, has a seriousness that cannot be missed. (The sketch was later included in *A Subtreasury of American Humor* [1941].) The parable, as White calls it, begins with a description of the simple life of the Pruitts, a family of fisherfolk living on a small island: "They liked the island and lived there from choice. In winter, when there wasn't much doing, they slept the clock around, like so many bears. In summer they dug clams and set off a few pinwheels and salutes on July 4th." One winter, alas, the water freezes: the marooned family can't use a boat and the ice is too treacherous to walk on. This would have been no misfortune—the Pruitts simply stay inside and play crokinole—but the outside world begins to worry about them, and help descends upon them like a plague. The army, the state police, Pathé news, reporters—all invade the island. Through a series of man-made disasters, the whole family but one is wiped out. The survivor, having buried his kin, leaves the island of his nativity.

The ultimate source of this parable of man's bumbling interference with his fellow man might have been a foolish performance White remembered from his college years. In the winter of 1920-21 three balloonists had been lost, and the rescue attempts read like a comedy. The men are saved and, disagreeing with each other, come out fighting. White had written an editorial on the affair, "The Belligerent Balloonists" (January 12, 1921). However, the immediate source of the parable was the rescue attempts on Tangier Island in the Chesapeake Bay, where some fifteen hundred inhabitants had been in real need of supplies. The matter had been reported in *The New York Times,* February 2-11, 1936.[11]

More than a statement about the corrupting and destructive effect of the complex world impinging on the lives of those living in happy simplicity, the parable concerns privacy as well. The Pruitts had lived as they chose to live, and their right to privacy had been invaded. Both themes are central to White's philosophy. Other themes he develops in *Every Day Is Saturday* involve politics, religion, progress, and, briefly, internationalism. It would have been difficult for a person writing in the 1930's not to become concerned, if not involved, with politics, for example, and White was no exception. But White, unlike many writers, belonged to no cults or groups; he was not a returning exile, nor a writer on the left. It has always been one of his qualities that he could remain an objective commentator; he was a "committed" writer, but always on his own terms. "There is a lot of the cat in me" he once wrote, "and cats are not joiners" (*One Man's Meat,* 159).

He writes in 1931 that "we happen to be, in a small way, on the other side of the fence from Father Coughlin on all his points" (*Every Day Is Saturday,* 70). On the other hand, about a year later, he chastizes the members of the John Reed Club for bad manners in their attack on Diego Rivera for "turning reactionary on them" (117). Capitalists, White adds, are at least polite. He could never accept the philosophy of "my country, right or wrong"; "We should like," he writes, "to be a good rebel, but it has always seemed to us difficult to be a rebel in this country, where there is nothing to rebel against except one's own stupidity in electing incompetent public officers and paying taxes on a standard of living far above the simple needs of life" (140).

Again, though he can consider Communism with some favor—"The truth is, we share many of the views held by the Communists and would join the party in a minute if we found them less snobbish"—he can at the same time remind the Communists that they are guilty of fuzzy thinking in pigeonholing people; they may flatteringly consider him a professional worker, but he is so only because "there are advertisers and businessmen footing the bill" *(Every Day Is Saturday,* 158, 159).

None of this is very serious political thinking; still, White was in a way testing his objectivity, his tolerance. He refused to be drawn in, and in retrospect he was perhaps closer to the truth politically than Theodore Dreiser, Sherwood Anderson, Malcolm Cowley, John Dos Passos, Edmund Wilson, Lincoln Steffens, Alfred Kreymborg, and Sidney Howard—the "literary leaders and converts" the Communists were, as he put it, licking their chops over *(Every Day Is Saturday,* 159).

White was skeptical, too, about religion and progress. He comments with mild irony on his feelings during a rare visit to church when Dr. Fosdick was preaching on the return of people to the Christian faith to do battle against atheism and agnosticism: "It stirred us to discover . . . that we were really part of a movement against irreligion, instead of just a mousy, faintly worried man, out wandering around the town on a Sunday morning" *(Every Day Is Saturday,* 224). In "Dr. Vinton," a sketch in *Quo Vadimus,* White takes a less innocent poke at religious self-righteousness and complacency. Dr. Vinton, the sole survivor of a disaster at sea, finds in his rescue a confirmation of his own exalted sense of virtue: he is saved by Providence, in order, apparently, to preach a fatuous sermon with a sea gull as its motif. There is a *Candide* touch in the essay, and doubts as to the ultimate wisdom of Providence linger in the reader's mind, and White's.

White was equally the mild protester against progress. One of the pleasantest parables in *Quo Vadimus* tells of Orville, a New York City sparrow with an inspired but pointless urge to tow a wren from Madison Square to 110th Street; Orville succeeds. The story is told without comment; however, in *Every Day Is Saturday* White had noted that "scientists assume that anything is progress just so long as it's never been accomplished before" (71). "The Crack of Doom," a more explicit comment, describes how progress has gradually reduced the earth to a shambles—the elms and willows have disappeared, rainfall has increased, and tropical storms have broken out with great intensity. New man-made diseases emerge and finally the earth, thrown off its course by the effect of radio waves, collides with a fixed star and goes up in flame. White concludes: "The light was noticed on Mars, where it brought a moment of pleasure to young lovers; for on Mars it is the custom to kiss one's beloved when a star falls" *(Quo Vadimus, 57)*.

White has written much more about progress and religion in some of his later essays. The comments in *Every Day Is Saturday* and *Quo Vadimus* are preliminary, as are his remarks about war and internationalism. Not until *The Wild Flag* (1946) do his ideas in these last areas receive their fullest development. Still, he wrote enough on the subject to indicate the direction of his thinking. "The Supremacy of Uruguay," for example, first published in 1933 and later included in *Quo Vadimus*, describes how Mr. Casablanca, an ingenious Uruguayan, has perfected a sound-making device which, by broadcasting an idiotic song at tremendous volume, can reduce whole populations to insanity. Inevitably Uruguay conquers the world; but, when she sends troops over the globe to occupy her domains, she meets no resistance anywhere; in fact, she is scarcely noticed: "Territorially her conquest was magnificent; politically, it was a fiasco" (39). Uruguayans are bored by their unchallenged supremacy, and the world as a whole lives in a fool's paradise of blissful peace and plenty. Inevitably, sanity returns: "land and sea forces were restored to fighting strength, and the avenging struggle was begun which eventually involved all the races of the earth, crushed Uruguay, and destroyed mankind without a trace" (40).

"Farewell, My Lovely!," one of White's best known essays, was published during this period, appearing first in *The New Yorker* of May 16, 1936; it was reprinted that same year in book form as *Farewell to Model T*, and has been reprinted in collections and anthologies a number of times since, including *A Second Tree from the Corner*. Suggested to White by a manuscript submitted to *The New Yorker* by Richard L. Strout, the   essay was published under the pseudonym Lee Strout White. It is essentially

White's, however, and belongs in the canon of his works. That he should publish it as he did was an act of generous consideration. White has stated a number of times, it should be observed, that many of his "Notes and Comment" items have been written on the hints and suggestions of others; he was not, however, able to acknowledge their help as he would have liked. He was likely pleased on this occasion to be able to acknowledge the help of another; a less conscientious writer might not have felt such an obligation.

The essay, a product of White's experience with his Model T, expresses as well his nostalgia for the past, for the Model T Ford was important in American history as well as in White's. "My own generation," he writes, "identifies it with Youth, with its gaudy, irretrievable excitements" (*The Second Tree from the Corner*, 32). With White, the identification was no so much with the gaudy excitement of youth as with his own private search for a role in life—a search that had its trials, but its vigor too: "The days were golden, the nights were dim and strange" (40).

The main part of the essay concerns two matters: first, the gadgets and attachments one could buy for a Model T; and, second, the almost mystic lore and legends associated with the car. For the first matter, Sears and Roebuck provided much; the Model T "was born naked as a baby, and a flourishing industry grew up out of correcting its rare deficiencies and combatting its fascinating diseases" (34). Of the lore and legends, more can be said, and White obviously delights in saying it. Of special interest is the timer, "an extravagantly odd little device, simple in construction, mysterious in function." You could hit it, blow on it, oil it; or even, as White tried once, spit on it—"You see," he writes, "the Model T driver moved in the realm of metaphysics. He believed his car could be hexed" (38). Beyond the fun, though, is accurate and close observation; White knew his car well, as a driver had to in those days.

A curious misprint in White's essay has become almost as elusive as the nature of the Model T itself. White had originally described the transmission of the Model T

as being, in part, "half metaphysics, half sheer friction"
(*The New Yorker*, 20). In the early reprintings, there was
no change; but, when the essay appeared in *The Second
Tree from the Corner*, the words were "half metaphysics,
half sheer fiction," and they have been turning up that way
ever since—in a 1962 reprinting, and in two 1966 reprintings. The mistake is an amiable one; it is the sort of thing
White *might* have written, and that may explain its per-
sistence. There is little point in mentioning it, except that
it seems amusingly attached to the legendary Model T.
Also, we should warn instructors teaching the essay (the
three reprintings mentioned are in collections designed
for college use) not to cite that particular phrase as an
example of White's stylistic precision.

In summary, from the late 1920's until 1938, White
had turned out many humorous pieces, had written count-
less newsbreak comments, and a major portion of the
"Notes and Comment" department of *The New Yorker*; in
addition, he had, with James Thurber, written amusingly
on the subject of sex. But more important, White was
well on his way to becoming the spokesman for a liter-
ate, cultured minority. He could see the seriousness of
the Depression; the follies and pretensions of politicians,
ministers, and scientists; the growing threat to civilization posed by an impending second world war—he could
see these things, and yet not lose his sense of humor, and
not be drawn into a dogmatic or doctrinaire position.
As he put it in *One Man's Meat*, "A writer must believe in
something, obviously, but he shouldn't join a club" (43).
He could speak for the troubled conservative who had
voted for Roosevelt and for the man who wanted social
progress without revolution—or without losing his individualism or his right to privacy. Above all, White spoke
for those who had not lost their sense of humor, for those
who could relish his jabs at Communist and Capitalist,
Democrat and Republican, thinker and buffoon, scientist
and charlatan alike. White had by now established himself,
and his best writing was yet to come.

CHAPTER *4*

# One Man's Meat:
# First Person Singular

WHY E. B. White left New York in the early part of 1938 and for five years lived on a farm on the Maine coast is a private matter. Still, since the change was important in his life, and had a considerable effect on his writing, we must be allowed to speculate. Perhaps, as Hyman suggested, he was on a "Thoreau jag" ("Urban New Yorker," 91); or perhaps, as Bishop said, he "went through some sort of inward upheaval," was tired of New York and his weekly paragraphs, and "was evidently trying to make contact with an outward and inward reality, such as Thoreau found by Walden Pond" (*One Man's Meat*, viii).[1] White told Robert Van Gelder that he felt he had to get away when he did "because there seemed less and less integrity . . . more people easing off on their principles for some little advantage" (*Writers and Writing*, 309). Or, it may be that, among other things, White wanted to take his son out of the private school he had been attending and let him experience for a while the more democratic atmosphere of a New England public school.

There was nothing very surprising, at any rate, in White's desire to move closer to the soil, to the outdoor life. Before college he had worked one summer on a farm in Hempstead, Long Island; he had always been fond of animals —the zoo was one of the places he liked in New York; he liked boats and salt water; and *Walden* really *was* one of his favorite books.

Whatever his reason for the move, two possibilities at least can be ruled out: he was not in rebellion against any restrictions on his writing by *The New Yorker* and he was not looking for an escape into an easy life of playing at farming. He told Roderick Nordell, for example, that he had never been asked to write in any particular way. *"The New Yorker,"* he said, "is a wonderful example of how a thing can succeed if you don't try to adjust" ("The Writer as a Private Man," 9). Although his contributions to *The New Yorker*, especially to "Notes and Comment," diminished during the Maine years, they did not cease. And no one reading *One Man's Meat* can imagine for a moment that the life was easy, either physically or intellectually. As Warren Beck comments, "Neither can his excursion into the pastoral life be judged escapist. Indeed, in 1938, the critical year of his retirement to Maine, he at once began to express in *Harper's* a realistic internationalism well ahead of *The New Yorker* and of lagging public opinion generally" (*College English*, 370). As for playing at being a farmer, nothing could be farther from the truth. Though White had help on his farm, he did a great deal of the work himself; at one time (October 1941) he was sending eighty dozen eggs a week to market.

It is true that White may have felt at times that he was cutting himself off too much. On the other hand—and this was no rebellion against restrictions on his writing for *The New Yorker*—he did, as he notes in the Foreword to the first edition of *One Man's Meat* (1942), enjoy using "I" (instead of the "We" of "Notes and Comment"), finding in the first person singular a closer link with his readers and with the times: "As a matter of fact," he says, "this quality in the book is a thing which perhaps gives it some relation to the war. It is a book of, for, and by an individual. In this respect it is anathema to our enemies, who find in individualism the signs of national decay" (vii). The sense of closeness to his readers lessened any possible feeling of isolation; when his farming activities became, after Pearl Harbor, more important, we can see an even greater closeness. In addition, he took to civil defense activities with seriousness and enthusiasm. White himself, in the Preface to the 1944 edition of *One Man's Meat*, has the best summary statement of his situation in Maine:

It is a collection of essays which I wrote from a salt water farm in Maine while engaged in trivial, peaceable pursuits, knowing all the time that the world hadn't arranged any true peace or granted anyone the privilege of indulging himself for long in trivialities. Although such a record is likely to seem incongruous, I see no harm in preserving it, the more so since I have begun to receive letters from soldiers overseas assuring me that there is a positive value to them in the memory of peace and home. (vii)

White did not leave New York without some regrets. Beneath the bathos of his Comment "The Departure of Eustace Tilley" (*The New Yorker*, August 7, 1937; reprinted, *The Second Tree from the Corner*), lay the truth that after ten years on *The New Yorker*, White found the break hard. White's next Comment was not until April 2, 1938; and he wrote scarcely half a dozen more for that year, and only fifteen or twenty for 1939 and for 1940.

"The Departure of Eustace Tilley" certainly is autobiographical. In a mock-interview, Tilley (a poignant and fanciful E. B. White) gives his reasons for leaving the city—for one thing, a cemetery where there are loudspeakers on the trees. In short, the invasion of the mechanical modern world is threatening to a man who loves the simple and the honest. "And then," says Tilley, "there are things I want to think about, things on which I can more readily concentrate when I'm not in town." And sounds—he wanted to hear the cock crow, "the wildest sound in all the world . . . I want to think about the custom of skiing in summertime, want to hear a child play thirds on the pianoforte in midafternoon. I shall devote considerable time to studying the faces of motorists drawn up for the red light; in their look of discontent is the answer to the industrial revolution" (*The Second Tree from the Corner*, 153). Tilley makes his final farewell as he leaves in a Victoria drawn by an old cob. After he leaves, the narrator turns away: "As we turned, we discovered to our surprise that the sidewalk, where he had paused a moment, was a pool of tears" (154).

1  *Stronger Statements, Deeper Convictions*

The first essay in *One Man's Meat* was written in July 1938; all but three of the essays in that collection appeared in the monthly "One Man's Meat" department of *Harper's Magazine*. The last essay in the first edition of *One Man's Meat* (1942) was written in December 1941; White added ten more essays to the 1944 edition.

The reader coming from *Quo Vadimus?* and *Every Day Is Saturday* to *One Man's Meat* is struck by White's greater sureness of material and expression, by his clearer thinking on many topics, and above all by his more penetrating moral purpose and his deeper conviction in attitudes and feelings. Not surprisingly he writes a good deal about his farming and related activities in Maine: chickens, sheep, fertilizer, the weather—these matters provide material for sometimes routine comments, and sometimes masterpieces of incisive and often beautiful evocations of pastoral simplicity and honesty. He also writes about many of the topics he had approached, often tentatively, in his earlier work. White at times really does seem to come closer to something solid and honest than anything he had been able to find in New York.

It isn't exactly privacy or simplicity that White finds in his own experience, although he has things to say about them. As a matter of fact, writing about the attention a person gets from his neighbors in a small community, White states that it is "necessary to come up to town after a long spell in the country, for a period of privacy and rest" (*One Man's Meat*, 55). But, he had discovered, there is a practical reason for the scrutiny a man gets from his neighbors in the country, and besides, if he learns to stare back, "the situation was instantly relieved." Anyway, keeping track of people was necessary: "It is a valuable personal intelligence service. I used to waste hours of time hunting up people who, if I'd used my eyes and ears, I should have known were some place else" (56).

Still, there was individualism; White liked the rural opposition that he noted to the 1940 Census, which included some questions not asked previously. This was a different sort of invasion of privacy: "The threat of a census has aroused the countryside because nobody looks forward with any pleasure to answering questions about his income or his bathtub. . . . Privacy, the abstract blessing, is a lot bigger than the average-sized tub. And, like a tub, it can be irreparably marred by a blow from a blunt instrument, or law" (147). Another blow against privacy that White did not like was the custom in some states of using automobile license plates for advertising. He objects to New York State's advertising the 1939 World's Fair and to Maine's inscribing "Vacationland" on its plates: "I believe the state is misusing its power in issuing license plates which are inscribed with a bit of institutional hoopla. . . . In effect this seemingly harmless practice makes every motorist an advance agent, without pay. It also gives some of us a touch of nausea" (148).

Progress, or the lack of it, continued to bother White; he sees a "dim degeneracy in progress" (35) that was particularly exemplified in automobile design: "I am fascinated by the anatomy of decline, by the spectacle of people passively accepting a degenerating process which is against their own interests" (186). Disheartening also is the "acceptance by other peoples of the strange modern governments which are destroying them in a dulcet fashion. I think there will some day be an awakening of a rude sort, just as there will some day inevitably be a union of democracies, after many millions have died for the treacherous design of nationalism" (189).

Two topics run through many of the essays: often stated, often implied, they exist as a unifying pattern for *One Man's Meat*. One concerns war and internationalism, and the other domestic social and political problems. White's growing concern about war and peace, his dedication to the ideal of world government, are discussed more fully in the chapter on *The Wild Flag*. A few examples from *One Man's Meat* show, however, the way White was continually relating his Maine activities to international affairs. In September 1938, he talks about a government pamphlet on culling chickens: "Isn't 'purge' the word they are groping for? Incidentally, this is one farm on which there will be no purge" (17). But, as his chicken farming became a more serious business, White had to give up such Quixotic humanitarianism.

In October 1938, he describes roofing his barn; but like a counterpoint, Munich is on his mind: "I'm down now; the barn is tight, and the peace is preserved. It is the ugliest peace the earth has ever received for a Christmas present" (20). "Coon-Hunt" is another example of this counterpoint effect. Before describing the coon-hunt itself, White talks about civil defense, and then he notes with some sharpness how the enemy had already made his presence felt. On Halloween, some junk had been piled up in front of a Jewish merchant's store. "The enemy," says White, "slipped into town and out again, and I think there were hardly a dozen people who caught the glimpse of his coat tails. . . . There would never be a moment, in war or in peace, when I wouldn't trade all the patriots in the county for one tolerant man" (267).

As a farmer, White came into closer contact with some aspects of the Roosevelt administration and the New Deal than did a good many academic theoreticians. In November 1940, he writes that he had some qualms about the three tons of free lime he had received from the government. He can accept the idea that the improvement of the soil is a benefit to the nation as a whole, but at the same time he feels "a slight sense of being under obligation to somebody" (195). And it doesn't prove that White is a conservative when he says, "I think that one hazard of the 'benefit' form of government is the likelihood that there will be an indefinite extension of benefits, each new one establishing an easy precedent for the next" (196).

In spite of White's jokingly attributing his compromising nature to hay fever—the source, also, he believed, of Daniel Webster's compromises—and his saying that his own political tendency was toward "the spineless middle ground" (9), he could, when Roosevelt suggested the limitation of incomes, approach the problem with imagination. The trouble with the profit system, he writes, "has always been that it was highly unprofitable to most people. The profits went to the few, the work went to the many" (339). This might have seemed to some *New Yorker* readers pure radicalism. Yet White's solution is moderate enough: what the ordinary man really wanted was a share in the profits. "He wanted the excitement of fluctuation, the agony of risk, the rewards of black ink. But nobody ever cut him in. . . . He worked and toiled, he sickened and died, but he never participated" (340). This may not have been sophisticated economic theory, but it was a personal and human statement. White himself tried the profit-sharing idea on a limited scale in *A Subtreasury of American Humor*. Almost all the contributors to the book, he said, were delighted with the arrangement (344).

It was too late, however, for that sort of social innovation, and the New Deal and governmental controls were there, for better or worse. It was sometimes worse, as far as White was concerned. In "Control" he expresses his annoyance at finding in his barn two men from the State who, without having asked permission, are giving his cows the Bang's test. He approves of the test, but he also thoroughly approves of "the old idea that a man's home is his castle and that anyone who arrives with a needle is expected to knock before entering" (337).

Self-imposed controls, however, were not necessarily better than those imposed by the government. For example, in January 1939, White objects to a writer who announced that owing to the seriousness of the times he would write nothing that wasn't "constructive and significant and liberty-loving" (42). To this ostentatious pronouncement, White replies that a writer must be free: "A literature composed of nothing but liberty-loving thoughts is little better than the propaganda which it seeks to defeat. . . . A despot doesn't fear eloquent writers preaching freedom— he fears a drunken poet who may crack a joke that will take hold" (43).

## II  *Three Pieces of Demolition, and "Once More to the Lake"*

Many of the essays in *One Man's Meat*, including most of those discussed so far, are made up of two or more fairly separate comments. Some of the best, however, are essays on a single topic; in these White achieves the highest level of his art. Three of them are effective pieces of demolition—of the New York World's Fair, or, as it was called then, The World of Tomorrow; of the Townsend Plan; and of Anne Lindbergh's book, *The Wave of the Future.*

The road to Tomorrow, says White, hitting his stride by the third paragraph of his essay "The World of Tomorrow," "leads through the chimney pots of Queens. It is a long, familiar journey, through Mulsified Shampoo and Mobilgas, through Bliss Street, Kix, Astring-O-Sol, and the Majestic Auto Seat Covers" (71). But White tries to be impartial: there are things of interest, even of beauty, at the fair. There is also an aseptic, impersonal quality, a vague uncertainty in the air, as if there was some doubt about the imminence of The World of Tomorrow, and a great dependence on microphones and loudspeakers: "In Tomorrow one voice does for all. But it is a little unsure of itself; it keeps testing itself; it says, 'Hello! One, two, three, four. Hello! One, two, three, four' " (75).

After an appealing description of a little boy who had won a free long-distance phone call at the telephone company building (the boy tried to call his father, but couldn't reach him), White epitomizes the fair with a description of a giant automaton, located outside of one of the "girlie" shows (where, with a neat compromise between morality and eroticism, the girls were allowed to expose one breast). Several girls sat on the robot's lap and were fondled by its huge rubber hands: "Here was the Fair, all fairs, in pantomime; and here the strange mixed dream that made the Fair: the heroic man, bloodless and perfect and enormous, created in his own image, and in his hand (rubber, aseptic) the literal desire, the warm and living breast" (79).

In August 1939, White reported on a talk given by Dr. Francis E. Townsend on the Townsend plan (a scheme, born of the Depression, to give a pension of two hundred dollars a month to all people over sixty by a tax of two per cent on the gross business of the country; the money was supposed to be spent within a month by the pensioner). The first part of the report is a sympathetic account of Townsend's talk—its simple appeal, the artless approach. "Maybe this Plan was it," writes White; "I never heard a milder-mannered economist, nor one more fully convinced of the right and wisdom of his proposal" (95). Of course, Townsend was far from artless; what gives the report its charm and its strength is *White's* apparent artlessness, as with beguiling innocence he begins to expose Townsend.

The shift in the report comes when White describes the question period after the talk: "It was at this point that Dr. Francis E. Townsend (of California) began quietly to come apart, like an inexpensive toy" (97). With a combination of calm reporting, gentle irony, and understatement, White deflates Townsend: "It spoiled his afternoon to be asked anything. Details of Townsendism were irksome in the extreme—he wanted to keep the Plan simple and beautiful, like young love before sex has reared its head. And now he was going to have to answer a lot of nasty old questions" (98). The piece ends with the housewives in the audience going back to their cooking (the talk had been given at a Methodist camp): "The vision of milk and honey, it comes and goes. But the odor of cooking goes on forever" (100).

Equally effective, and somewhat sharper in tone, is White's critical attack on Anne Lindbergh's book, *The Wave of the Future*. As in his treatment of Townsend, White is fair. Anne Lindbergh, he says "wants a good world, as I do," but "she has retreated into the pure realm of thought, leaving the rest of us to rassle with the bear" (204). Her thesis was that the "wave of the future" was the new social and economic forces being exploited in Germany, Russia, and Italy. These forces had been used badly at times, she conceded; but they are the hope for a new world. White then moves in, with more vigor than he had shown against Townsend, and with good reason—for the issue was far more important, the antagonist more formidable.

These forces, says White, are not new at all: they are "the backwash of the past," and have "muddied the world for centuries" (205). Mrs. Lindbergh had argued that the

new forces had emerged from the distresses of the people,
and were therefore somehow good. White attacks this
assumption:

> The fascist ideal, however great the misery which released it and
> however impressive the self-denial and the burning courage
> which promote it, does not hold the seed of a better order but of
> a worse one, and it always has a foul smell and a bad effect on
> the soil. It stank at the time of Christ and it stinks today, wher-
> ever you find it and in whatever form, big or little—even here in
> America, the little fascists always at their tricks, stirring up a
> lynching mob or flagellating the devil or selling a sex pamphlet
> to tired, bewildered old men. The forces are always the same—
> on the people's side frustration, disaffection; on the leader's side
> control of hysteria, perversion of information, abandonment of
> principle. (206)

Careful not to accuse Mrs. Lindbergh of being a Fascist,
White is bothered not only by what she has written but
also by the popularity of her ideas; for this was a time
when, in certain circles in England and America, Fascism
had disturbingly enthusiastic partisans—Mussolini had,
after all, made the trains run on time; and both he and
Hitler were far more efficient than the bumbling democracies—so the clichés went. Many people had spoken
of the book, White notes; they would say that, though
they had reservations about it, " 'there's something to what
she says just the same' " (209). This "something" White
tries to find and cannot. His faith in freedom and democracy—a naïve faith, some might have said then, and would
say today—was not easily shaken.

Seen in the context of 1940, White's attack on the *Wave
of the Future* was more significant than readers of today
might suppose. The native Fascist movement had considerable strength and had recently been encouraged by the
growing popularity of the America First movement, which
though not Fascist, had the support of some Fascist groups.
Huey Long was dead; but there were others, like William
Dudley Pelley, Gerald B. Winrod, Lawrence Dennis, and

Father Coughlin. Hitler was by no means universally de-
spised in America, for his "accomplishments" drew admiration from some; and the subsurface anti-semitism
in many Americans, and the Anglophobia in others, found
encouragement in Fascist doctrines. The native Fascist
movement appealed, not because it was Fascist so much
as because it was isolationist, anti-Communist, and often
virulently anti-Roosevelt. According to Raymond Gram
Swing, Father Coughlin, at the height of his popularity
(this was a few years before the *Wave of the Future*), was
receiving more mail than any other man in America,
"averaging for a long period about 80,000 letters a week"
(*Forerunners of American Fascism,* 40).

The best essay in *One Man's Meat*, "Once More to the
Lake," combines in rare form White's stylistic economy,
which is essentially the stuff of poetry, with his skillful
use of details, his gift for the evocation of the past and his
feeling of the circularity of time; and, finally, his haunt-
ing awareness of the transient quality of life, the imminence of death. In the essay, simple in subject though not in
form, White recounts a week's visit he made with his son
to a Maine lake where he himself had vacationed as a
child with his parents. During this week's visit White
walked and fished with his son, and in many ways lived
again the days of his childhood: there was the same excitement at arrival, the same early mornings at the lake, the
same cottage with partitions that did not go up to the
ceiling, the same kind of farmhouse meals, the same lake,
the same kind of people visiting, the same questions, the
same thunderstorms, and the same swimming in the rain
afterwards.

This is the material of the essay, but it is not the essay.
Some of the chief values lie in the rhythmic alternations
between past and present, and in the feeling of duality
in White, both father and son at the same time. The essay
opens with a reference to the summer of 1904, when White
began coming to the lake with his father. The second paragraph describes White returning to the lake, bringing
his son with him, and speculating on the changes that may
have taken place—"I wondered how time would have

marred this unique, this holy spot" (246). White then moves to a reverie about the past, how it was when he had visited the lake as a boy, and especially the early morning remoteness, and the cathedral-like stillness.

From this recollection of the past, the essay shifts again to the present. Now, an intrusion of the present upon the past, a tarred road leads toward the lake. But this change is not profound, and White almost imperceptibly slips back into being at once his son and his father: "I began to sustain the illusion that he was I, and therefore, by simple transposition, that I was my father. . . . I seemed to be living a dual existence. . . . It gave me a creepy sensation" (247-48). The last sentence is typically White—before the situation becomes too involved, too philosophical, or too serious, he lightens the tone with a colloquialism. After all, this was a summer vacation.

He goes fishing with his son, and past and present merge: "Everything was as it always had been . . . the years were a mirage and there had been no years . . . I looked at the boy . . . and it was my hands that held his rod, my eyes watching" (248). Emphasizing the lack of change, the blending of time, was the tideless lake: a constancy strange to a man used to salt water, but a detail beautifully consistent with the theme. Other details—and there are no extraneous ones in this sketch—reinforce the timelessness of the scene: the same sticks in the water; the minnows swimming by, with their shadows on the clear sand beneath, "doubling the attendance, so clear and sharp in the sunlight"; and always the same bather, "this cultist," washing himself with a cake of soap (248-49).

White then shifts to the present: there are two tracks in the road now, not the old three, where the horse made a path down the middle; this was not a jarring note, though, and other details emerge and once again the past and present blend. The arrival by train and wagon years ago, the arrival now by car—that was different; but the emotions of arrival, they were the same. Then the one real break from the past, the one really jarring note enters: the outboard motors instead of the old, quieter inboards. The new sounds are "petulant," "whining"; and, slipping back

into the past again, White recalls the skill needed to operate the old-style motors.

Then, as the rhythm of the essay asserts itself, the blend
again of past and present, and again White's sense of duality
with his son. The unity, the circularity, of time is epitomized
by the thunderstorm that comes up over the lake: the same
rumbles, the same rain afterwards, the same swimmers
in the rain, and the same jokes about getting wet, "linking
the generations in a strong indestructible chain" (253).

But at the end, beautifully worked out, the tone suddenly shifts. White's son, going in swimming during the rain,
gets his dripping trunks from the line and puts them on: "I
watched him, his hard little body, skinny and bare, saw
him wince slightly as he pulled up around his vitals the
small, soggy, icy garment. As he buckled the swollen
belt suddenly my groin felt the chill of death" (253). Age
and death are present with frightening vividness, and
time suddenly seems to reverse itself, for White is no
longer young and in the past. Because the aura of death
surrounds his son as well as himself, the generations
are linked again, but in mortality, not in life.

We find in this essay much of the credo of E. B. White.
Here is his simple love of nature; his nostalgia for the past,
and along with that his inclination (never quite given
in to) to reject the present (the tarred road, the outboard
motors) in favor of the past; his preference for doing rather
than thinking (the walking, the fishing, the boating); his
feeling for the mystery outside the church, not inside it
("this holy spot," "cathedral stillness"); his vivid language,
with his liking for the simple, natural figures of speech
("the boat would leap ahead, charging bullfashion at the
dock"); his love for people, for his son, and his sense of
identity with the young (which made him such a good
writer, later on, of children's stories); and the everpresent
sense of death that with White was sometimes whimsical—
Thurber said, "He expects every day of his life that something will kill him: a bit of mold, a small bug, a piece of
huckleberry pie" ("E.B.W.," p. 9)—and sometimes intensely serious: his poem "The Cornfield" ends with these
lines:

And being present at the birth
Of my child's wonderment at earth,
I felt my own life stir again
By the still graveyard of the grain.

Above all, we find here White's sense of reality, a sense so deceptively off-hand at times that many readers could be misled and think of White as a pale modern Thoreau who is revisiting Walden, echoing his master, and escaping from the world with a happy phrase or two. But there is nothing in this essay, or in *One Man's Meat* that, carefully read, would support such a view, and plenty exists to refute it. The ending of "Once More to the Lake" shows White seeing life steadily and seeing it whole; and perhaps the ending looks forward to the time a year or so later when White returned to full-time work with *The New Yorker*, and, with the essays from *The New Yorker* that make up *The Wild Flag*, to a closer identification with the forces that were changing the world.

## III  *American Humor*

Before White returned to New York, he completed another project: his editing, with the help of his wife, of *A Subtreasury of American Humor* (1941). The anthology was popular: it was a Book-of-the-Month-Club selection; in abridged form, an Armed Services edition; and later, also in abridged form, a Pocket Book edition. The Whites interpreted the term "humor" broadly, and the anthology contained such things as the first chapter of *Babbit* and a *New Yorker* "Profile" of Father Divine, an item more disturbing than funny (it was omitted in the abridged editions). There was a wide selection of items; and, though some readers might have found some favorites missing, most readers, I suspect, would have found some pleasant things they had *not* known about. Anthologies present problems, and omissions are sometimes the result of copyright complications, not a reflection of the taste or knowledge of the editor. The selections in this collection, at any rate, reveal a more than casual acquaintance with literature

on the part of the Whites, and relatively little of it has become dated.

But the most important part of *A Subtreasury of American
Humor* was the Preface by E. B. White. He explains the
criteria for the selection of the items, and talks about humor.
The Preface has been reprinted, in a slightly changed form, in
*The Second Tree from the Corner*, in *The Comic in Theory
and Practice* (1960),[2] and in *An E. B. White Reader* (1966).
In making the selections, says White, he and his wife
rejected the goal of inclusiveness: "We asked simply
that we be amused, now in 1941" (xiv). Some areas of humor,
White notes, were not represented at all: no joke-book
stuff, radio humor, or comic-strip material. Also missing
was something the editors had originally wanted to put
in—newspaper humor. What they could find wasn't funny
any more, though White's description of their efforts to
find it was funny enough. You finally, he says, locate
some newspaper piece that was supposed to be funny: "You
coax the library into letting you examine this immortal
yet crumbling relic, this sere and yellow specimen, and
as it trickles into your lap, particle by particle, you read
with glassy eyes and set jaw the howlingly funny news
story of long ago. It is a bad moment" (xiii).

White begins his discussion of the nature of humor with
some valuable and original comments on dialect and illiter-
acies. Petroleum Nasby's misspellings for humorous effect,
for example, pose a problem to White. Nasby uses "uv"
for "of," and "offis" for "office," to cite two examples.
White notes that he himself pronounces "of" and "office"
as if they were "uv" and "offis"; thus, he concludes, the
humorous effect is not from the odd pronunciations but
from the funny spellings themselves—as if the character
involved were writing, not speaking. But then, as White
says, no one who could write at all would write "uv."
And in Streeter's *Dere Mable*, which clearly involves
characters writing, not speaking, it is unlikely that anyone would consistently leave off the "g" in "-ing" words.
White concludes that "the popularity of all dialect stuff
derives in part from flattery of the reader—giving him a
pleasant sensation of superiority which he gets from work-

ing out the intricacies of misspelling, and the satisfaction of detecting boorishness or illiteracy in someone else" (xv).

White is perfectly well aware that this "dialect stuff" is a surface matter; the real nature of humor lies deeper and has a certain "fragility, an evasiveness," which is beyond analysis. It is not that humorists are really sad people, sad clowns; rather, "there is a deep vein of melancholy running through everyone's life and . . . a humorist, perhaps more sensible of it than some others, compensates for it actively and positively" (xviii). The humorist thus comes close to the truth of human experience, but there is an irony in being a humorist—the world patronizes him: "It decorates its serious artists with laurel, and its wags with Brussels sprouts" (xviii). The humorist must learn to live with a kind of injustice; he must put up with his friends who will ask the question every humorist is asked: When are you "going to write something serious"? (xix). But the real problem is the conflict between high emotion and the temptation or danger of ending with a snicker:

Here, then, is the very nub of the conflict: the careful form of art, and the careless shape of life itself. What a man does with this uninvited snicker (which may closely resemble a sob, at that) decides his destiny. If he resists it, conceals it, destroys it, he may keep his architectural scheme intact and save his building, and the world will never know. If he gives in to it, he becomes a humorist, and the sharp brim of the fool's cap leaves a mark forever on his brow. (xix)

The comments are perceptive, and perhaps defensive; for White, particularly in his earlier days, was considered by many to be mostly a humorist. He was that, but never exclusively so. Often he did give in to the temptation and throw his cap in the reader's face, but just as often he did not. Still, there is no great need to classify; it is possible to combine high emotion, a deep moral purpose, with a sense of humor—as Charles Dickens and Thomas Hardy have done. If not quite in this company, White is not too far away from them in spirit and in his perception that there is more than one way to the truth.

Typical of White's critical writing, the Preface is neither profound nor scholarly; yet, clear, refreshing, funny at times, it probably comes as close to the truth as most of what has been written on the subject. I don't know whether White has read Sigmund Freud, Henri Bergson, or George Meredith on humor; he does say that "analysts have had their go at humor, and I have read some of this interpretive literature, but without being greatly instructed" (xvii). It took a certain amount of courage to admit this, but he was not writing for an academic audience and had no need to establish his credentials. He could be humorous himself, and he could recognize humor in the writings of others. That was enough.

CHAPTER *5*

## "The Answer to War is No War"

### I  *Background*

IN the last item in *One Man's Meat*, written in January 1943, White describes one of his geese that had left the flock for a while and then returned, but still seemed separated from the rest: "I imagine something of this sort would happen if I were to return to the city. . . . I'm not sure you can ever go back even if you should want to" (349). He did, however, return to New York later that same year but without giving up his Maine farm (he returned to full-time residence in Maine in 1957); and he resumed active participation on *The New Yorker*, chiefly as a writer for "Notes and Comment." Actually, White had started contributing extensively again to "Notes and Comment" in 1942. In 1941, he contributed only two items; in 1942, over fifty; and in 1943, sixty or so—even in that year, however, his contributions did not equal those he had made in the years before 1937, when he often wrote most if not all of the department.

The war was the main reason for White's return to New York and to *The New Yorker*. He wrote on subjects other than war, peace, and the need for world government, but his editorials on these topics were among the most important of his writings from 1943 to 1945. (White, accurately enough, called his articles "editorials"; with a few exceptions, they were published as part of the "Notes and Comment" department.)

We can sense a restlessness in the *One Man's Meat* essays written after Pearl Harbor; White wanted to be nearer the center of things than he was in Maine, and with some of *The New Yorker* staff in the armed forces, he would have been needed more than ever by Ross, the editor of *The New Yorker*. Of course, in New York he still felt out of the war: he speaks of "the uneasy chair of civil life" (*The Wild Flag*, 54); and in January 1944, in a sketch about an operation he had, he mentions trying to spare the nurses by waiting on himself: "I enjoyed the nonsensical sensation of being in contact with the enemy" (*The Second Tree from the Corner*, 6). It was partly this uneasiness, this lack of direct involvement, that gave tension and vigor to his editorials.

White had been thinking about the problems of war and world peace long before these years, however; in his high school days he had been something of an isolationist and skeptical about an enduring peace. He wrote in the Mount Vernon High School *Oracle* for January-February 1917, that "a strong sentiment seems to prevail against becoming mixed up in other people's affairs. That's the right idea, say we" (15). When the United States got into the war, White's attitude changed; and he was more or less conventionally patriotic, but not very hopeful about the prospects of world peace. In *One Man's Meat*, he quotes from his journal for February 18, 1918: "The talk is of Universal Peace after the war—everlasting peace through the medium of an international council. Nations will be ruled by brotherly love and divine principle, arms will be laid down forever and man will return to the ploughshare. Bosh!" (112).

White's was the healthy skepticism of a college freshman; he wasn't always that pessimistic. He wrote little about the League of Nations while he was editor of the *Sun*, but he did touch on it and on the subject of disarmament. A General Bullard, who had spoken against disarmament, cited as an argument his experience in the Philippines, where he had observed monkeys using sticks as weapons. "It is a significant fact," said the General, "that from the monkey to the American the state

of their culture corresponded exactly to the state of their
armament. The monkeys that, in the struggle of life, had
sense enough to pick up and use a stick as an arm, developed into men. The others remained monkeys."
White's comment—he had quoted Bullard in a *Sun* editorial—is: "Yes, and what monkeys the men have made
out of themselves with their arms. Bullard is perhaps
a better general than philosopher" (February 24, 1921).

By the end of the 1920's, White's ideas began to take
shape. *Every Day Is Saturday* opens with a Comment
for January 7, 1928: "Lately we've been on the watch
for some semblance of unity in the affairs of the spinning
world, some identifiable rhythm. None has appeared" (1).
A few years later, he is more hopeful. Referring to Father
Coughlin's pronouncement that internationalism would
be our ruin, White says that "talking against internationalism over the radio is like talking against rain in a rainstorm;
the radio has made internationalism a fact, it has made
boundaries look so silly that we wonder how mapmakers
can draw maps without laughing" (70).

Five months later, in October 1931, White mentions
*What Are We to Do with Our Lives?* by H. G. Wells:
"[Wells] would teach school children to regard the world
as a planet instead of as a battleground; he would modern-
ize religion, making it reasonable rather than realistic
. . . he would put an end to war by creating a commonweal. Unless we go ahead with these general Utopian
principles, he promises, civilization will go to pieces.
We think he is probably right. . . . Just now, it looks
as though we might all die fighting for the principle of the
renunciation of war as an instrument of national policy"
(*Every Day Is Saturday*, 93). The influence of H. G. Wells
in the 1920's and 1930's was pervasive, and it certainly
touched White, who refers to Wells in *The Wild Flag* (133-34).
Wells had recommended a world government, not a union of
nations; this recommendation was White's central thesis in
*The Wild Flag.* In fact, one statement by Wells in *The World
of William Clissold* (1926) could almost have been written
by White. Wells said of the League of Nations that "everybody in council and assembly alike was there as a na-

tional partisan. Nobody represented mankind" (580). Wells had also stated that "the open conspiracy" (the title of one of his earlier books and his term for the new forces that were bringing about a world commonwealth) was an active militant force, disrespectful of nationality: "There is no reason why it should tolerate noxious or obstructive governments because they hold their own in this or that patch of human territory." The English-speaking nations, Wells continued, plus France, Germany, Holland, Scandinavia, and Russia, could cease to arm against each other, and "impose disarmament and a respect for human freedom in every corner of the  planet. It is fantastic pedantry to wait for all the world to accede before all the world is pacified and policed" *(What Are We to Do with Our Lives?*, 137-38).

This statement is very close to what White says in *One Man's Meat*, June 1940: "The armies of the democracies which will lead up to my world state will be built *for attack. . . .* But their minds will not be on conquest nor will they confuse raw materials with the good life. They will be trained to attack today's injustice, rather than to repel tomorrow's invasion" (161-62). Both White and Wells are on tricky ground here—just how tricky, American Viet Nam policy has made clear.

White writes elsewhere in *One Man's Meat* about world government. Noting how changing designs of cars are forced upon us against our best interests, he predicts an awakening "of a rude sort, just as there will some day inevitably be a union of democracies, after many millions have died for the treacherous design of nationalism" (189). In another essay, he describes his interviewing some tourists in a trailer camp in Florida; he was pleased to discover a four-to-three sentiment in favor of a union of democracies. In June 1941, he comments on a suggestion by Bertrand Russell that there be an alliance or league of nations: "I had rather see an attempt at union than an attempt at an alliance, for then the participants would be bound in fact rather than in words" (244).

After Pearl Harbor, he writes in *One Man's Meat*, "Who is there big enough to love the whole planet? We must find such people for the next society" (276). Such a group, he adds, (with certainly unconscious irony) might be the scientists (Wells had suggested something like this) who are "preoccupied with an atom, not an atoll" (276).

## II   The Wild Flag

White, then, had begun to formulate his thoughts about internationalism and world government well before the time of *The Wild Flag* editorials. He has said that his comments about world government did not truly represent the position of *The New Yorker* as a whole, and that Ross thought him a "visionary";[1] however, the magazine could not have been wholly unreceptive either. For years, during the 1930's, *The New Yorker* had been running full-page World Peaceways advertisements (the magazine donated the space) which set before the reader, often in striking and dramatic ways, the hope of a world united in peace. White, in fact, devoted part of a comment on August 4, 1945, to a discussion of one of those advertisements.

By 1943, the subject of world unity, of world government, of world federalism—the terms are many—was widely discussed. White had spoken warmly of Wendell Wilkie's *One World* (1943). He hadn't found it particularly well written, but he says, "The title of Wendell Wilkie's book turned out to be an astonishingly electrifying phrase. Millions were shaken by it."[2] White had also praised Emery Reves's *A Democratic Manifesto* (1942). Of the many other works on the subject, a few more might be mentioned: Clarence Streit's *Union Now* (shorter edition, 1940), and Arthur Millspaugh's *Peace Plans and American Choices* (1942). The most popular book on the subject, Emery Reves's *The Anatomy of Peace*, was not published until 1945.

In his Preface to *The Wild Flag*,[3] White admits the difficulty of achieving his goal of world government; but he believes the case for it worth stating anyway. Men would have to learn to expand their loyalties to include more than a "stream in Devonshire," and world government would deprive men of the "enormous personal satisfaction of distrusting what he doesn't know and despising what he has never seen. . . . The awful truth is, a world government would lack an enemy" (xi, xii). But he feels there isn't much time for choice, and he finds a few hopeful signs. For one, in a cosmopolis like New York City he sees a world government on a small scale; for another, he thinks that war has "reached a new low in the esteem of all people" (xiii). He also concedes that he was too theoretical for the statesman, and "too sweetly reasonable" for the skeptic. The Preface gives an accurate summation of White's views, and perhaps an indication of some of his weaknesses; it tells little, however, of the eloquence and variety in the statement of those views.

In many respects repetitious—for White has really only one theme—*The Wild Flag* has more variety than might at first be supposed. For example, there are fairly clear, though not formal, divisions in the book: the editorials before the United Nations Conference in San Francisco, those from that time until the explosion of the atomic bomb in Hiroshima, and those after that.

White approaches his theme in several ways in the first part of *The Wild Flag*. For one, he shows the inadequacies of any social or political organization based on the existence of nation-states as separate, sovereign powers. We can deplore, he says, the execution of American pilots, but we cannot talk as if international law or some abstract "justice" were involved. The first step in getting international law "is to realize with dazzling clearness, that we haven't got it and never have had it" (7). Nor can we continue to speak of foreign "policy" and "self-interest" as intelligent approaches to international affairs. As long as each nation pursues its own policy, its own self-interest, there will be conflict.

Another approach White uses with considerable flourish and effectiveness is to single out those individuals or groups opposing any sort of world unity. The Daughters of the American Revolution, for example, with what White calls its "enviable record of consistency" (4), resolved to oppose any political union involving the United States that would deprive this country of free and independent action. The organization also opposed any proposals that would destroy the sovereignty of Americans; and finally, it went on record to assert that the main American objective was to be victorious in the shortest possible time. Rejecting each of these points, White concludes: "That's three strikes on the Daughters of the American Revolution, who are swinging wide at the fastbreaking curves of war. Ladies, you're out!" (4). He also had fine scorn for Clarence Buddington Kelland's view that the Pacific Ocean must become an American lake. White, mentioning the Sea of Okhotsk, the Sea of Japan, the Yellow Sea, the South China Sea, concludes: "Are these the coves in an American lake—little bays where we can go to catch pickerel among the weeds?" (18). Finally, he turns his scorn on the twenty-three House members who, in the fall of 1943, voted against the Fulbright resolution, a measure designed to strenthen the emerging United Nations.

This sort of attack, however, does not form the main substance of any part of *The Wild Flag*. Mostly, White comments on some current event and relates it to the need for world government. Thus, at the time of the Dumbarton Oaks meeting, White quotes Sir Alexander Cadogan, head of the British group, who said that the nations of the world should maintain forces for joint action to keep the peace. The point, says White, was not to have joint action available—it didn't help against the rise of Fascism in the 1920's, for example—but "to make world government available so that action won't have to be joint" (37).

Finally, White spends some time relating to his readers the hopeful signs he sees. When the name "United Nations" is chosen at Dumbarton Oaks for the proposed international organization, White finds the term misleading, as there wasn't to be any real union; still, it was a start. He finds another sign of hope in the Allied victories in 1944 and, during the Battle of the Bulge, in the spirit shown by the Allied armies. He several times praises Governor Harold Stassen, who had spoken out for world government; and, repeating a point he had made in the Preface, he finds still another sign of encouragement in the evidence he sees that war itself was becoming increasingly unpopular.

At the time of the San Francisco Conference to complete

a charter for the United Nations Organization, White
played a dual role—he continued his editorial contributions on world government to *The New Yorker*, and also
served as his magazine's reporter at large in San Francisco.
From May 1945, until his first editorial on world government
after the first atomic bomb explosion in Japan (August
6, 1945), he showed some skepticism about the new organization but, at the same time, an undercurrent of optimism.

The first sound of life at San Francisco, according to White,
was T. V. Soong's declaration that China was prepared to
yield part of her sovereignty in the interests of collec-
tive security. This offer ran counter to what White felt
had been the prevailing tone at San Francisco—the desire
to *preserve* sovereignty. White had apparently carried
his *Walden* with him to San Francisco, for at the end of his
comment on Soong, he quotes from Chapter XV ("fifteenth
chapter, second verse") a passage Thoreau had written
about the sound of concord to be heard amidst the discordant sounds of nature. And discordant sounds there
were in San Francisco: the noise, for example, about what to
do with dictatorships like Argentina that had been on the
"right side" during the war.

The goals of the United Nations, White objects, are
"far in advance of any machinery yet proposed for bringing them to life" (89). In one somewhat cynical comment he
proposes that the United Nations be located in Dinosaur
Park, South Dakota, "so that earnest statesmen, glancing
up from their secret instructions from the home office,
may gaze out upon the prehistoric sovereigns who kept
on fighting one another until they perished from the earth"
(96). Yet, he hopes that the United States Senate will
ratify the charter, after which the best thing Americans
can do is set about improving the United Nations.

In his two "Reporter at Large" reports for *The New
Yorker*, White, more leisurely in his comments, spends
some time on background material. In both reports, however, we see the same tentative hopefulness: if "justice,
law, and human rights still had no effective international
status, at least they were being written into the proceedings" (May 12, 1945, 42). And in both reports White speaks

strongly about the urgency of the conference where, he says, the sense of "destiny and the sense of obligation . . . haunts the citadel" (May 5, 1945, 47).

If White felt a sense of urgency at the time of the San Francisco conference, he felt it with more intensity after August 6, 1945, when an atomic bomb was dropped on Hiroshima. In his editorial for August 18, 1945, he repeats his complaint that the political plans for the post-war world are not "fantastic" enough. He adds that recent events have made the meetings at San Francisco "seem like the preparations some little girls might make for a lawn party as a thunderhead gathers just beyond the garden gate" (109).

Several editorials in this last part of *The Wild Flag* involve a matter that White had only touched on earlier—the problem of war criminals. Though he questions the legality of the Nuremberg trials, he finds the very existence of them "exciting because they are the unconscious expression of the universal desire for a broader legal structure, and hence for a higher social structure" (117). White was drawn into the trials himself in a curious way. He wrote on October 20, 1945, that Captain Wintman, the defense attorney at Nuremberg, had challenged the legality of the trials and in support had quoted a *New Yorker* editorial for September 15, 1945. White was not mentioned, but he had written the editorial. White read in *The New York Times* of October 9, 1945, that Wintman had quoted the following from *The New Yorker:* "We strongly suspect a long delay in the war trials, not so much because there is no solid floor under a certain court room as because there is no foundation under the new level of justice with which the victorious nations are now fumbling. . . . The chief thing to remember about international law is that it is not law and has never worked" (3). The quotation had been slightly mangled, but it was accurate in the main.

Somewhat surprised, perhaps, to find his words used to defend the Nazis, White nonetheless stuck to his point: "These so-called war trials can be magnificent if they can be made to clarify rather than cloud this issue; they will be extremely valuable as precedents if they are presented as a preview of the justice that may some day exist, not as an example of the justice that we have on hand" (120).

The final entry in *The Wild Flag*, June 1, 1946, is a mixture of hope and disappointment. White traces the failure of the Allies to achieve the beginnings of a world government back to the Atlantic Charter and the Dumbarton Oaks meeting, and he concedes that the world is not ready for government on a planetary scale: "In our opinion it will never be ready. The test is whether the people will chance it anyway" (185). He recognizes that at the moment we lack the leadership to bring the dream into reality; but, if we fail, he concludes, "science will have won the day, and the people can retire from the field, to lie down with the dinosaur and the heath hen—who didn't belong here either, apparently" (188).

### III  *Critique*

Written over a period of three years, the editorials in *The Wild Flag* are White's only book-length discussion of a single topic. They form some of his best writing; because of the subject, however, they must be judged on somewhat different grounds from that of his other work—and judging them today is not easy. If the book seems naïve, the reader must remember the context—World War II—and the often naïve hopes many people had for world peace. If it is repetitious, he must remember that originally the editorials appeared at uneven intervals over an extended period of time. Some years later White himself was not especially enthusiastic about the book. It was, he told Roderick Nordell, "a little uninformed and half-baked. . . . We had no conception at that time of what the Soviet Union would do."[4] At its publication, *The Wild Flag* had both favorable and unfavorable reviews, including a scathing notice in *The Nation*.

It is easy to state that the book lacks political and historical background, as well as psychological and anthropological insights. In addition, White is not entirely clear as to what he means by world government. He speaks at one time of the "super-state" (43), and elsewhere of "federal union" (148). That he wished to see the end of the present nation-state society is clear enough, however; but, writing with almost no mention of the past, White seems at times too far removed from the necessary realities—the social and economic obstacles to the creation of a world state. The problem is that what might have been out of place in an editorial becomes necessary in a book. Certainly references to earlier periods in human history when some semblance of unity was achieved would have given White's views more perspective. There is probably something to be learned from the experiences of the Romans, from the medieval attempts at synthesis, from the *philosophes* of the eighteenth century, or from the British "peace" of the nineteenth.

Perhaps more serious than White's lack of historical perspective is the absence of any reference to the psychological and sociological aspects of war. When he sees a hopeful sign in the dislike of war by the soldiers of World War II, he is not convincing. No one knows why men fight, but certainly some account must be taken of the theories that see war as an aspect of human nature, as a result of displaced resentment against parents, or as growing out of our competitive society, and so on.[5] Many people dislike war, but just as many seem, consciously or otherwise, to like or need it. This does not mean that White is wrong to be hopeful that wars will cease, but it does mean that we must be guarded about judgments based on the surface unpopularity of any given war. We must face Flugel's discouraging statement that "war provides the most thoroughgoing and morally satisfactory rationalization for unsocial conduct that has yet been discovered."[6]

It is easy, as I said, to make these points. They must be made, but they do not comprise the whole truth. White was not alone in the battle for world government; a number of books had been published that could provide the reader with the background, the depth, missing in *The Wild Flag*.[7] There was a need for the clear and simple statement of White's book; a need for a writer who could, at the very moment that he was in fact ignoring the complexities, praise Reves's *A Democratic Manifesto*, and conclude on the homey and not inaccurate note that it "shows sovereignty up for a dead cat" (4). Also, it might be added, there was need for someone like White, who, true to his convictions, spoke as an independent. White, much as he may have been in sympathy with groups like the United World Federalists, did not become personally associated with them or with any other organized groups. He spoke as an individual, and his words had a personal conviction, with none of the canned quality of the organized appeal.

There is a need for idealism, for theory, for the statement that is "too sweetly reasonable." We can argue whether serious and scholarly studies produce the right climate of opinion, or whether the right climate of opinion makes the serious studies effective. Both are necessary, of course; and, if the popularizing idealist runs the risk of setting expectations too high, the more serious study may be ignored. It is impossible to judge the effect of *The Wild Flag*, but it may be that some *New Yorker* readers began to accept a point of view they might not have encountered in so palatable a form elsewhere. I can testify for myself and a number of others that reading *The Wild Flag* editorials overseas in the "pony edition" of *The New Yorker* provided hope and inspiration.

Even if in some ways White lacked profundity, he made a number of good observations and made them clearly. Disarmament, security leagues, treaties—all these attempts at securing peace, he said, have been and will be futile. Unless men can achieve real union, unless each nation-state can agree to relinquish some of its sovereignty, unless there can be a real basis for what we like to call international law and justice, unless, finally, men's loyalties can extend beyond those they feel for their own particular piece of territory, we have little hope. We have to have the world view; the machinery can come later. Without the world view, White had concluded, we would indeed join the dinosaurs and the heath hens.

White's own retrospective comment on *The Wild Flag*,

made a few years before the interview with Nordell, is an
honest and valid summation: "The book was rather dreamy
and uninformed, but it was good-spirited . . . and I still
think that what I said was essentially sound, although
I'm not sure the timing was right."[8]

CHAPTER *6*

# Stories for Children

"We wove a web in childhood,
A Web of sunny air . . . ."

*Charlotte Brontë*

### I   Stuart Little

IN October 1964, White told Susan Frank of the Cornell
*Sun* why he wrote *Stuart Little* and *Charlotte's Web:*
"I couldn't tell stories to children and they always were
after me to tell them a story and I found I couldn't do it.
So I had to get it down on paper" (S8). White added to
the explanation in an article in *The New York Times,*
(March 6, 1966) after a televised version of *Stuart Little.*
The story began, he said, with a dream he had had in the late
1920's of a "small character who had the features of a
mouse, was nicely dressed, courageous, and questing"
(Sec. X, 19). After the dream, White wrote a number of
episodes about the mouse, whom he named Stuart, to
tell to demanding nephews and nieces—of whom, he said,
he had eighteen. In 1938, White sent the episodes to a
publisher to see if they would be acceptable if expanded.
They were not; but some years later, in the winter of
1944-45, he finished *Stuart Little,* which was then accepted by Harper and Brothers.

In an essay about children's books in *One Man's Meat,*
White had speculated that it must be "a lot of fun to write

for children—reasonably easy work, perhaps even important work" (25). And he apparently did enjoy it; "They're
lots of fun," he told Howard Cushman, after he had finished *Charlotte's Web*.[1] White may have found some relief
from the tensions of the war years when he turned back
to *Stuart Little;* in addition, the story seemed an expression of nostalgia for the past, for the simplicity and fantasies of childhood, and for the rural setting of the last and
best part of the story.

White's wife had for a number of years reviewed children's
books, and at times many of them were around his house;
thus he had opportunities to see what was being written. He
expressed in his *One Man's Meat* essay, by the way, a mild
distaste for the amount of geographical and linguistic
information being purveyed to children that year (1938);
*Stuart Little, Charlotte's Web,* and *The Trumpet of the
Swan* are refreshingly free of studied attempts to improve
young minds. What makes White's three books outstanding
is that he has written them in the classical tradition of
children's stories—in the tradition of Lewis Carroll's *Alice
in Wonderland,* Mary Molesworth's *The Cuckoo Clock,*
Kenneth Grahame's *The Wind in the Willows,* A.A. Milne's
*Winnie the Pooh.* There is much to be learned from White's
stories, to be sure, but it is not geography, or science, or
even the habits of mice and pigs. What the child does learn
—and what children learn from the other fine children's
books—is a great deal about loyalty, honesty, love, sadness,
and happiness.

The use of animals is so traditional in children's stories
that we need not look much beyond White's dream for
sources of *Stuart Little.* One of his earliest published
works had been about a dog; he had liked animals as a
child and continued to like them as an adult; one of his
favorite works was Don Marquis's *archy and mehitabel*
(the cat Snowbell in *Stuart Little* has some faint echoes
of Mehitabel). In general, White uses the standard elements of classic stories: talking animals, the mingling of
animals and humans on almost equal terms, the blending
of fantasy and reality. Not so traditional is his having
Stuart, a mouse, the child of human parents.

On the whole, the three books are not particularly innovative, but they are unusual for White in that they represent his longest sustained work. He has not written many long pieces; in fact, he said in the Foreword to *The Second Tree from the Corner* that he was a "man unable to sit still for more than a few minutes at a time, untouched by the dedication required for sustained literary endeavor, yet unable *not* to write" (xii). The structure of *Stuart Little* reveals the weaknesses we might expect in a writer disinclined or unable to write extensively on any one subject; these weaknesses, however, are absent in the other two books.

*Stuart Little* opens with a matter-of-fact approach to the unusual proposition that human parents (the Littles) could produce a mouse as their second son. Before he was many days old, Stuart not only looked like a mouse, he acted like one, "wearing a gray hat and carrying a small cane" (2). This suggestion of the dandy, however, is dropped, and we hear little more of the hat and cane; except for his size, Stuart is like any boy. Maturing rapidly enough to dispense with the usual infancy, he begins his adventures almost at once in the Little's New York City home. He is helpful, because of his smallness, in getting a ring out of the sink drain. Mr. Little, curious about new things and far-away places, asks how it was. "It was all right," said Stuart, in crisp Hemingway style. But Stuart is not a tough guy, and his adventures are those that happen because of his size.

Stuart never really fits in at the Littles. Their first son, George, is not a companion, and Snowbell the cat is more an adversary than a friend. Before the coming of the bird Margalo, Stuart's biggest adventure is participating in the sailboat race in Central Park. Stuart, sailing a model boat, comes into his own, and the story loses for a while its somewhat episodic character. And Stuart begins to be more like E. B. White, especially in his liking for the water: "He was an adventurous little fellow and loved the feel of the breeze in his face and the cry of the gulls overhead and the heave of the great swell under him" (31). As Stuart, so far as we know, had not been to sea, his reactions seem rather sudden and not precisely appropriate to Central Park—but they are expressive enough of White's love of the sea.

With the arrival of Margalo, the story takes a new direction and a new unity. After a few more adventures of the earlier sort, Margalo disappears. From that point on, the story is different; for Stuart, who is determined to find her, leaves home with no word to the Littles of his intentions and becomes the independent hero. His adventures now have direction and purpose, though like the traditional fairy-tale hero, Stuart is sidetracked several times and once is tempted to settle down. He resists the temptation, however, and continues on his quest for Margalo.

Having obtained a small car and begun his search, Stuart's next adventure is one of the best in the book—his teaching Miss Gunderson's class in Number Seven School in a town he passes through. Stuart sets the tone for the scene when he explains to his pupils what was the matter with Miss Gunderson: "Vitamin trouble . . . . She took Vitamin D when she needed A. She took B when she was short of C, and her system became overloaded with riboflavin, thiamine hydrochloride, and even with pyridoxine, the need for which in human nutrition has not been established" (89). In other words, she was suffering, generally, from the complexities of our pseudo-scientific society and, specifically, from reading too many cereal-box labels.

Stuart's conduct of the class is an admirable exercise in the elimination of the superfluous in education. Grasping his lapels in both hands to look like a professor (and reminding us of White's description of Professor Strunk), Stuart takes full control: he skips arithmetic, tells his pupils to use a dictionary for spelling, finds that they can already write, and says that he has never heard of social studies. When the class turns to conversation, Stuart (whose creator was still writing *The Wild Flag* editorials) introduces the subject of the "King of the World," later modifying this title to "Chairman of the World." What follows is not quite what Malcolm Cowley has suggested,[2] a fable about the

San Francisco Conference (White had finished *Stuart Little* before it occurred), but an instructive statement by Stuart about world law: "Nix on swiping anything," and "absolutely no being mean" (93, 94). Stuart acts as temporary world chairman; his only problem is that, much taken by a balsam pillow belonging to one of his pupils, he has to resist a strong urge to run off with it.

Stuart is tempted to settle down when, at Ames's Crossing, he discovers Harriet Ames, a pretty girl his own size. He writes a charmingly adolescent letter asking for a date, and he spends agonizing hours planning and day-dreaming until she arrives. But the date is a failure—Stuart's canoe is ruined, the evening on the river is spoiled, Stuart refuses to be comforted, and they part, Stuart continuing on his search for Margalo. He never finds her, but he is headed north, which he feels is the right direction. This ending has puzzled some children, and it may be partly what bothered Anne Carroll Moore, children's librarian emeritus of the New York Public Library, who told White that the story was, as he recalled her words, "nonaffirmative, inconclusive, unfit for children."[3] She may have been bothered as well by Stuart's origin from human parents, though it is hard to see why.

It is a risky business to find depths of meaning, mythic overtones, and other complexities, in children's stories; and it is with a clear awareness of the dangers that I suggest that in *Stuart Little* one may find amusing and interesting autobiographical elements. Stuart Little shares not only White's love of sailing but also the wandering uncertainty White felt in his first years after college. We are tempted to draw a parallel between Stuart's car and White's Model T; moreover, both White and Stuart seem to have been motivated in their wanderings by the same impulse —Stuart, in talking about Harriet Ames to the storekeeper, explains that he is not much of a society man now: "Too much on the move. I never stay long anywhere—I blow into a town and blow right out again, here today, gone tomorrow, a will o' the wisp" (104). Stuart may remind some readers of the sea-faring rat in Kenneth Grahame's *The Wind in the Willows,* but he also sounds like White talking about his post-college days: "I was rather young to be so far north, but there is a period near the beginning of every man's life when he has little to cling to except his unmanageable dream, little to support him except good health, and nowhere to go but all over the place" (*The Points of My Compass,* 205). At the end of the story Stuart too is headed north, looking for Margalo, *his* dream.

Another part of the story that suggests White's youth is what Stuart finds at the general store at Ames's Crossing where he stops for a drink of sarsaparilla. The man has not only that but also "root beer, birch beer, ginger ale, Moxie, lemon soda, Coca Cola, Pepsi Cola, Dipsi Cola, Pipsi Cola, Popsi Cola" (102). This interesting bill of fare is partly in fun, but partly an old-fashioned one that belongs in *White's* youth, not Stuart Little's. In "Once More to the Lake," White spoke of going to the store with his son; now, he said, "there was more Coca Cola and not so much Moxie and root beer and birch beer and sarsaparilla" (*One Man's Meat,* 252).

Stuart's encounter with Harriet Ames certainly reminds us of those tenuous, transient encounters—in a restaurant, skating—that White has described about himself. When Stuart Little had to change his shirt three times while waiting for Harriet because he was perspiring so much, we recall White's description of his date with Parnell Thomas's sister: "The emotional strain of the afternoon had caused me to perspire uninterruptedly" (*The Second Tree from the Corner,* 22).

What these parallels suggest—if the reader is willing to grant that they suggest anything—is that at some point in the composition of *Stuart Little,* perhaps when White resumed writing the story in the winter of 1944-45, it became quite different from what it had been at the start. White simply dropped the earlier part of the story—George, the Littles, Snowbell, and Stuart with hat and cane—and added something much better. For he made Stuart the embodiment not just of his own early restlessness but of the restlessness and the yearning that come at some point in many people's lives. However, in making the story nostalgically touching to the adult reader, he has, perhaps, made it inconclusive for some children.

*Stuart Little* has continued, nonetheless, to be popular with children and adults; but Cowley was right when he observed the parts were greater than the whole.[4] White surpassed his first success in children's stories with *Charlotte's Web,* where there is far more unity, and where the ending, though partly sad, leaves the child with the central questions answered and with confidence in the continuity of life.

## II   Charlotte's Web

*Stuart Little* had a long gestation in White's mind, and he has talked about it in print at some length. He has published little about the composition of *Charlotte's Web*; however, it is clear from a letter by White,[5] and from the manuscript versions of the story in the E. B. White collection at Cornell University, that he had difficulties in writing it. Most important, perhaps, is that in its early version, Fern, an essential character, is absent.

More conventional in its conception than *Stuart Little,* the story begins with a problem White had faced himself — what to do with the weak animals on a farm. At first White, as a chicken farmer, had humanely asserted (in opposition to the ways of dictators) that there would be no culling, or purging, of weak stock on his farm. Later, when he had to face the reality of farming as a business, he weeded out the weaklings like any farmer. In the opening of *Charlotte's Web,* Fern Zuckerman protests the elimination of the runt piglet; she wants "justice," and her father cannot resist her pleas. Fern adopts the pig, names him Wilbur, and thinks about him in school as an older girl might think about a boy.

*Charlotte's Web* thus opens on a much more realistic level than *Stuart Little*; there is, in fact, an underlying realism throughout the story. Fern, an important part of this realism, is vital to the story. Wilbur and Charlotte, however, are the central characters. In spite of Fern's occasional company,

Wilbur is lonely. Templeton, the rat, is no playmate; Wilbur, looking for a friend, discovers Charlotte, a spider. He is, naturally, a little uneasy about her, for a spider's life, as Charlotte says later, "can't help being something of a mess" (164). Wilbur, however, was "merely suffering the doubts and fears that often go with finding a new friend" (41).

As Wilbur and Charlotte's friendship develops, Fern moves into the background; Templeton, the other important character, becomes a sort of anti-hero, a shrewd tough guy, and at times a comedian. When he is rolling a rotten goose egg, he reassures Charlotte: " 'I won't break it,' snarled Templeton. 'I know what I'm doing. I handle stuff like this all the time' " (47). Templeton is interesting; more subtly drawn than most of the characters in *Stuart Little*, he is not evil—he does, indeed, perform, for selfish reasons, some useful services for Wilbur—yet he has a disturbing baseness about him. And, like some shrewd and calculating people, he has at times a beguiling directness and even eloquence.

By the first fifty pages or so, the  plot is set: Wilbur has learned that he is fated to be killed, and Charlotte has promised to save him. Fern knows about all this, yet she is curiously inactive. When her brother Avery tries to capture Charlotte, for example, Fern tells him to stop; but she does nothing more, and it is only the accident of Avery's falling on Templeton's rotten egg, and the ensuing odor, that causes enough confusion to save Charlotte. Fern, however, has a function here: as the spectator, she supplies an element of continuity; she also serves as a link between the animal and the human world.

Charlotte's first act in saving Wilbur is to spin a web with the words "SOME PIG!" woven in it, attracting wide attention to Wilbur. Mrs. Zuckerman objects that it is not the pig but the spider that is unusual: " 'Oh, no,' said Zuckerman. 'It's the pig that's unusual' " (81). After this truth, with White reminding us of the human tendency to be amazed at the wrong things, the people scarcely mention the spider. Another point for the adult is White's gently satirical comment that on the Sunday after "SOME PIG!"

had appeared, the minister "explained" the miracle, saying that "the words on the spider's web proved that human beings must always be on the watch for the coming of wonders" (85).

Fern continues her passive role of spectator and listener. One day, however, she hears Charlotte tell a story about a cousin of hers who had caught a fish in her web. Fern tells the story to her mother, who, disturbed not only by the amount of time Fern has been spending in the barn, but also by Fern's saying that Charlotte can talk, takes her to see old Doctor Dorian, who does not provide exactly the satisfaction Mrs. Zuckerman had hoped for. For one thing, he points out what everyone else had missed—that *any* spider's web is a miracle. Then he reassures Mrs. Zuckerman: "if Fern says animals talk—well, perhaps they do." He also suggests that, although he himself might feel that spiders and pigs were as important as Henry Fussy (a boy Fern knows), the day will come when Henry will attract Fern more than spiders and pigs. Thus, Fern is for a moment brought to the forefront again, and her emerging maturity suggested.

Another change is foreshadowed in the next chapter when we learn that Charlotte "had worries of her own" (115), and might not be able to go with Wilbur to the approaching County Fair. Her egg-laying time is approaching, though White does not yet reveal the full implications of that event. The change in Fern, however, begins to appear quite soon. When preparations are being made for the Fair, Fern puts on her prettiest dress and thinks of the boys she will see. Later, at the climax of Wilbur's activities in the Fair, Fern is almost separated from the main action. When it is discovered that another pig has won first prize, Fern asks for some money so she can go to the midway. A few moments later, when the announcement has has been made that Wilbur is to be brought to the judge's booth for a special award, Fern again asks for money, this time for herself and Henry. When the Zuckermans drive with Wilbur to the judge's booth, they pass the Ferris wheel. Fern looks up at it, wishing she were there with Henry. Finally, just before Wilbur gets his prize, Fern races away in search of Henry; she has forgotten Wilbur.

Wilbur, too famous a pig to be killed, is saved; the rest of the story is Charlotte's. She has given birth to her eggs, made her egg sack, and is waiting for death. She will be dead before the return to the farm, and the most Wilbur can do is save her egg sack which, with the grudging help of Templeton, he does. Charlotte is left behind; "No one was with her when she died" (171). But the eggs hatch the next spring; a few spiders, new Charlottes, stay with Wilbur; and every year the cycle is repeated. Fern is out of it. "She was growing up, and was careful to avoid childish things" (183).

The story is touching, with death and sadness, but also continuity and renewal. The main story—the saving of Wilbur and Charlotte's death—has clear progress; what helps to give it additional depth and unity is Fern, who is really the key to the structure. It is ironic that Fern is absent when Wilbur reaches his highest triumph, and when Charlotte dies. Yet, given the real-life situation of Fern, her absence is almost inevitable. She is no stock figure for the telling of the story, or for getting the attention of the young reader, although a child can identify with her. She is a girl growing up, and her growth is a counterpoint to the main plot.

White doesn't dwell on Fern's growth, and we should not try, any more than in *Stuart Little*, to find profundity and complication where none exists. I doubt if most children think much about Fern at the last; their attention is on Wilbur and Charlotte. Still, every good children's story has something for the adult as well as for the child, and Fern is part of the story for the adult. With Wilbur and the yearly spring-born spiders, the world of childhood continues; with Fern there is growth and transition to a world where it is not the spider's life, but man's, that can't help being something of a mess. It is also a world where the miracle of love and courtship supplements the miracle of the spider's web.

The *Trumpet of the Swan*, published in 1970, is in some ways a curious combination of *Stuart Little* and *Charlotte's Web*. Louis the swan has adventures in Boston and Philadelphia that remind us of Stuart's wanderings; at the same time, the relation between Sam Beaver, a boy moving into the adult world, and Louis is a little like that between Fern and Wilbur. But the book never reaches the level of the first two. Some familiar White themes are there—the delicate father-son relationship, the pleasure in animals and nature, the beauty and truth of love— yet there is something missing. What can and cannot be done in fantasy is hard to define; perhaps a swan's playing a trumpet in a night club, or breaking through a plate-glass window with only a minor injury, is harder to accept than Stuart's or Wilbur's adventures, I don't know. Certainly *The Trumpet of the Swan* is a success; for another writer it might have been a triumph.

E. B. White's first two children's books have become classics. Bennett Cerf wrote that if there is any "book of the current season still in active circulation fifty years hence, it will be *Charlotte's Web*."[6] The three books are White's longest sustained efforts; in *Stuart Little* there were problems of unity; *Charlotte's Web* has a near-perfect structure. White has not been given to long works, but here he found a medium that was congenial to him, and it may well be that he will be longest remembered for these stories, particularly *Charlotte's Web*. It would be a fate by no means ironic or dismaying, and he would be in good company.

What White has done in these stories is to write clearly and simply, as he has always done; to be free from the bondage of current events that has dated many of his *New Yorker* pieces; and to be independent of the pressure of literary trends and fads. Of course, White has always been in the best tradition of literature—of stylistic excellence, of clarity, of simple eloquence. What could be better, for example, than Templeton's description of his revel at the Fair: " 'What a night!' he repeated hoarsely. 'What feasting and carousing! A real gorge! I must have eaten the remains of thirty lunches. Never have I seen such leavings, and everything well-ripened and seasoned with the passage of time and the heat of the day. Oh it was rich, my friends, rich!' " (148).

Above all, White has put into these stories in unalloyed form his compassion and humanity; his delight in the physical world; his feeling for the reality and importance of the small and simple ambitions of small and simple people; his faith in dreams and in the continuity of affection and love.

CHAPTER 7

# Past, Present, and Future:
# Some "Bizarre Thoughts"

### I  *Introductions*

IN the years between *One Man's Meat* (Second Edition, 1944), and *The Second Tree from the Corner* (1954), White, in addition to the works discussed in chapters V and VI, wrote *Here Is New York* (1949) and the introductions to two books. He also continued writing tag-lines for newsbreaks, contributed to "Notes and Comment," and wrote a number of poems, stories, and sketches, mostly for *The New Yorker*; some of these were later collected in *The Second Tree from the Corner*. The two introductions, reprinted with a few minor changes in *The Second Tree from the Corner*, were to *A Basic Chicken Guide for the Small Flock Owner* (1944) by Roy Jones, and the 1950 edition of *the lives and times of archy and mehitabel* by Don Marquis.

The introduction to *A Basic Chicken Guide*, which reflects the experience White had gained in raising chickens in Maine, has the peculiar distinction of having been written before he had read the book; that there were few contradictions between White's advice to chicken owners and what Jones had to say would suggest that White knew his subject well. True, White instructs his readers never to give day-old chicks starter mash for the first couple of days, and Jones advises starting them with mash and chick-feed, but no reader would have been in trouble following White's advice. The one or two other bits of contradictory advice were equally minor.

Of particular value in the introduction are the humorous but nonetheless useful warnings to the neophyte who, after reading White's words, would enter the business of raising chickens seriously and without the illusion that it was a simple, easy way of getting fresh eggs for breakfast. He would also enter the business aware that it had its rewards and even, implausibly enough, its poetry. White concludes his introduction by quoting Clarence Day's "Oh who that ever lived and loved/Can look upon an egg unmoved?" and then adding: "Reader, if you can look upon an egg unmoved, stay away from hens" *(The Second Tree from the Corner,* 239).

The introduction to Don Marquis's *archy and mehitabel* is more serious and without doubt closer to White's heart, for he had a deep affection for Don Marquis and a profound understanding of his creative problems. White sees a parallel between the cockroach hurling himself at the typewriter keys in order to hammer out his work, then falling exhausted to the floor, and the pain creative work exacted from Marquis: "After about a lifetime of frightfully difficult literary labor keeping newspapers supplied with copy, he fell exhausted" *(The Second Tree from the Corner,* 182).

The idea of a cockroach jumping head down on the keys and leaving free-verse messages in a typewriter was, says White, a "lucky accident" that fitted the particular creative needs of Marquis, who found his column tiring work. The creation of Archy, White goes on, allowed Marquis to use short lines, suited to his one-column newspaper format; "at the same time it allowed his spirit to soar while viewing things from the under side, insect fashion" (184).

White makes of Archy something of a symbol for literary creativity: "He cast himself with all his force upon a key, head downward. So do we all." Marquis was dogged by the question, is "the stuff literature or not?" This, admits White, is the question that "dogs us all." Behind his analysis lay a sympathy and admiration for Marquis; for White, like Marquis in one way at least, also found it hard to write sustained work—and he might have felt that he

too, by a lucky accident, had found his ideal medium in
*The New Yorker.* In addition, White, through his admiration
for the craft of Don Marquis, shows something less than
admiration for the kind of columnist that succeeded Marquis
and others of his era. "Nowadays," White says, "to get
a columning job a man need only have the soul of a Peep Tom
or a third-rate prophet. There are plenty of loud clowns
and bad poets at work on papers today, but there are not
many columnists adding to belles lettres, and certainly
there is no Don Marquis at work on any big daily."

White has always had great respect for the serious creative artist, and Don Marquis had been one of those writers
White admired when he came to New York after Seattle and
Alaska. Thus, White's tribute has something of that nostalgia
for the past so frequent in his work. He concludes his introduction: "I am deeply sensible of what it meant to be a
young man when Archy was at the top of his form and when
Marquis was discussing the Almost Perfect State in the
daily paper. Buying a paper then was quietly exciting, in
a way that it has ceased to be." In the case of Marquis,
White's nostalgic tribute was neither idealized nor sen-
timental; and if the Introduction tells us again about White's
sensitive admiration for the good and the honest in art,
it also reminds us, if we need reminding, that *archy and
mehitabel* has a distinguished place in American literature.

## II   *New York City*

White's tribute to his city, *Here Is New York*, was first
published in *Holiday* (April 1949) and later that year
in book form by Harper and Brothers. The book, or rather
long essay—it is only forty-five pages—reveals as much
about E. B. White as about New York; it helps to account for
his love of New York, just as *One Man's Meat* does for his
love of Maine. To the reader of White's poetry and his
early *New Yorker* pieces, there are a number of familiar observations about the city in *Here Is New York*, and a few
new ones. All are made with eloquence and in a kind of
final form, for the book is not just an explanation of New
York, but a plea for it.

One of the main things White liked about New York was its "gift of privacy." Many of the stories and anecdotes told about White, especially those concerning his early *New Yorker* years—his eating alone, his escaping from strangers and sneaking out of parties—testify to this gift. New York, he observes in *Here Is New York*, blends privacy "with the excitement of participation; and better than most dense communities it succeeds in insulating the individual (if he wants it, and almost everybody wants or needs it) against all enormous and violent and wonderful events that are taking place every minute" (13). Granting that many New Yorkers come there to escape reality, he notes that creativity demands the foregoing of distractions; and though New York can be lonely, the city also has the power of imparting rejuvenation. To White there are three New Yorks. The first two, the New York of the man born there, and that of the commuter, he did not find especially interesting; the New York of the people who were "born somewhere else and came . . . in quest of something" is the important city, and these are the people who give it passion (17).

White is neither innocent nor naïve when he talks about his city. Russell Maloney, a year or so before *Here Is New York*, had written, quite inaccurately, that White regarded the city "fondly, like a spinster looking at her tank of guppies."[1] In truth, White sees clearly the implausible balance that keeps the city going. "Long ago," he writes, it "should have experienced an insoluble traffic snarl and some impossible bottleneck" (24). He notes too the uneasy balance of tolerance and prejudice: "If the people were to depart even briefly from the peace of cosmopolitan intercourse, the town would blow up higher than a kite" (43). He is also aware of the ability of New Yorkers to resist panic and mass hysteria (the great blackout of 1965 showed that White was right).

It can be argued with justice that White was less aware of the problems of the blacks than some observers of the city. However, in 1948 relatively few non-blacks saw how bad the problem was, and it is easy to judge with the advantage of hindsight. White does see that the blacks found

difficulty in getting jobs, and he is certainly right that hous-
ing is a major part of the problem. The situation was simply more urgent and complex than many observers could
see in 1948. The blacks form no real part of the New York
that White describes.

White does observe, nonetheless, that there has been
an increasing tension and irritability during the years
he has known New York; and in 1948 the threat of atomic
destruction hung over the city. He pleads for peace, and
ends his book with the observation that there is a willow
tree in an interior garden near the United Nations headquarters: "Whenever I look at it nowadays, and feel the cold
shadow of the planes, I think: 'This must be saved, this
particular thing, this very tree.' If it were to go, all would
go—this city, this mischievous and marvelous monument
which not to look upon would be like death" (54).

### III  *America: "Progress" and Good Intentions*

*The Second Tree from the Corner* was published in 1954;
the title story, "The Second Tree from the Corner," was
first published in 1947, two years before *Here Is New
York,* which ended, as we have seen, with White's using a
willow tree near the United Nations as a symbol of what
must be saved from the threat of war and destruction.
This symbol suggests the theme of a good many of the
pieces in *The Second Tree from the Corner,* especially the
more recent ones: the theme, that is, that deals with the
paradox of modern man, the threats to his civilization,
and the hope that something, at least, can be preserved
of his culture. The best of these pieces include the title
story, "The Door," "The Decline of Sport," "The Morning of the Day They Did It," and "The Hour of Letdown."

The weakest section of the book, "Shop Talk," is a
selection from the "Notes and Comment" Department of
*The New Yorker;* many of these belong to an earlier period. The sort of thing represented in *Every Day Is Saturday,* they are often dated; the exceptions are the sharp
and still relevant jabs at some abuse, some current id-
iocy: the critic who rejects a play he hasn't seen, the pred-

atory photographer who waits for the suicide to jump, and the vulnerability and conceit of those who talk glibly about English usage and ignore "the broncolike ability of the English language to throw whoever leaps cocksurely into the saddle" (166).

Another section, "Notes on the City," also largely a selection of earlier pieces, shows White to be the sensitive, warm, but somehow not fully involved observer of the city. Two items here stand above the rest. One, "Life in Bomb Shadow" (Jan. 20, 1951), analyzes soberly life in New York under the threat of atomic war. There are, says White, three groups of people in New York: those who cannot leave because of lack of money; those who have decided to leave; and those who can leave, but have chosen to stay. The first and third groups are very large; White puts himself in the third. He concludes, "The only way to dwell in cities these days, whether it be wise or foolish, is in the conviction that the city itself is a monument of one's own making, to which each shall be faithful in his own fashion" (231). This piece and one about the United Nations—White still maintained his faith in that organization, in spite of its manifest weaknesses, its "interminable debates"—may suggest that White's view of New York, if not naïve, is at least limited. To be fair, however, we should note that in the late 1940's and early 1950's, relatively few people saw the American city as it is seen today.

That White linked the fate of the United Nations with New York was perfectly reasonable. For White, New York was a microcosm that would ultimately share the fate of the world outside—and that fate hinged on the United Nations. But, forthright as White's almost romantic affection and loyalty for New York were, they were never tinged with either the official ballyhoo that accompanied the New York World's Fair, 1964-65, or the phoniness of the term "fun city."

One thing that always colored White's view of New York was his tendency to see it in terms of his own past: as the place of his early questings and of the beginnings of his success. This tendency is clear in "The Hotel of the Total Stranger," a sketch or parable about the city which opens with a Mr. Volente taking a taxi to the Hotel of the Total Stranger and thinking about the room before he checks in, seeing it in all its sterile comfort and conformity. Then, with a technique White employs a number of times, Mr. Volente's thoughts and recollections go back to the past, before the moment of checking in. Through Mr. Volente, White evokes his own nostalgic feelings about New York: "That was the thing about New York, it was always bringing up something out of your past, something ridiculous or lovely or glistening" (213). For example, Mr. Volente recalled the time a waitress had spilled buttermilk on his blue suit. That was in fact the incident that got White started on his career with *The New Yorker* (see above, Chapter One).

The chief value of the sketch is the light it sheds on White and his early years in New York, making vivid his fears, doubts, and uncertainties. But that is not its only value, for it stands alone as a tone poem on New York and the city's power to absorb and store all emotions, all feelings, from despair to hope to success. Furthermore, the title evokes hauntingly the paradoxical way the city has of presenting one with the flux of life (the little world of the "hotel") and at the same time providing anonymity and privacy.

Several other sketches in *The Second Tree from the Corner* illustrate what White calls in the Foreword his "tendency to revisit." One, "Speaking of Counterweights" goes back to his days on the *Seattle Times*, and the ride he took on the odd little car around the top of the building in preparation for a feature story. Apparently the story was never published; *The Seattle Times* for June 2, 1923, carried two pictures of the counter-weight vehicle but nothing else about it. It is an amusing account, though the experience, with White perched precariously over the edge of the roof, was unnerving enough at the time. It was in that sketch that White quotes the words of John, the city editor, who advised him when he was stuck for a way to express something, to "just say the words" (12).

Another recollection of the past, written later than this sketch, but referring to an earlier period in White's

life, is "Afternoon of an American Boy," an account of
White's hesitant, teen-age entry into the world of dating.
He had taken the sister of Parnell Thomas to a tea-dance
at the Plaza Hotel in New York. At the time White published the sketch (November 29, 1947), Thomas was Chairman of the House Un-American Activities Committee, and
White makes the needling suggestion that perhaps his
own ineptitude in dating was un-American. But, except for a
comment or two, the sketch does not attack the committee.

Lacking the perceptions of James Joyce, say, or Katherine
Mansfield, White nonetheless skillfully evokes the poig-
gnancy and innocence of youth; it was the sort of experience
that many a reader might recall for himself. He ends the
account: "But there must be millions of aging males, now
slipping into their anecdotage, who recall their Willie
Baxter period with affection, and who remember some
similar journey into ineptitude, in that precious, brief
moment in life before love's pages, through constant
reference, had become dog-eared, and before its narra-
tive, through sheer competence, had lost the first, wild
sense of derring-do" (23).

The best of *The Second Tree from the Corner* are the
selections dealing with the quandary, the paradox, of
modern man—those that show White's skepticism about
science and progress. He had written on these matters
before, but some of his strongest statements and his best
work are here; a number of short pieces can serve as an introduction to the longer ones. In "The Dream of the American Male" (July 19, 1941), White sets forth clearly and
simply the paradox of modern man. A *Life* article had stated
that Dorothy Lamour was the woman most desired by army
men. Taking off from this, White expounds on man's desire
for the simple and the unadorned: "Now, in the final complexity of an age which has reached its highest expression
in the instrument panel of a long-range bomber, it is a good
idea to remember that Man's most persistent dream is of a
forest pool and a girl coming out of it unashamed."

In another piece White salutes Mrs. Wienkus, a woman
arrested by the police in Newark, New Jersey, because
she slept in two empty cartons in a hallway. She has a

bank account of $19,799.09, but she has managed to escape the "conveniences" of life, like the "coat hangers in the closet and the cord that pulls the light and the dish that holds the soap and the mirror that conceals the cabinet where lives the aspirin that kills the pain."

In still another Comment, December 24, 1949, White notes the essential simplicity of Christmas: "Christmas in this year of crisis must compete as never before with the dazzling complexity of man, whose tangential desires and ingenuities have created a world that gives any simple thing the look of obsolescence—as though there were something inherently foolish in what is simple, or natural." And in "Air Raid Drill" (December 8, 1951), White observes that the building where he works (and where there was an air-raid drill) has no thirteenth floor. It would be well, he concludes, if the scientists who had invented the A-bomb had waited "until the rest of us could look the number 13 square in the face."

But White's attitude towards complexity and progress was ambiguous. In "Heavier than Air" (Feb. 16, 1952), he comments almost with relief on a letter from an airline pilot who *was* adjusted to modern life and had what White called a "serene personality." White then confesses his own dualism: half the time he is "blissfully wedded to the modern scene," and half the time "the fusspot moralist suspicious of all progress." Still, it was just this ambiguity in the modern scene that bothered him as it had bothered thoughtful sceptics from long before the time of Jonathan Swift and Voltaire: the spectacle of man's potential for good combined with his stupidity and his proclivity for evil.

All of these shorter items have touched on the basic theme of *The Second Tree from the Corner*, a theme developed in more detail and with more artistry in a number of longer pieces, the first of which, "The Door" (March 25, 1939), has become one of White's best-known stories. In "The Door," White makes extensive use of two matters recently discussed in articles in *The New York Times* (February and March 1939) and in *Life* (March 6, 1939). The *Times* articles were reports about a model-home exhibit in Rockefeller Center, and the one from *Life* about the effects of frustration in some experiments on rats. He also used some other briefer items from *Time* and *The New York Times,* as William R. Steinhoff has shown in a perceptive article on the story.[2] White's use of contemporary material, of course, was characteristic, growing out of his long habit of using such material in his *New Yorker* "Notes and Comment."

"The Door" has little plot in the conventional sense, but it has a structure that derives from White's use of the *Times* and *Life* articles. The central character, the "he" of the story, is being shown through an exhibit of a model house, (everything in the house had been tested and could be laundered); and, as he is taken through, he compares himself to rats in a laboratory. That the house was being exhibited in Rockefeller Center fits the theme of the story, for such a situation is as artificial and incongruous as modern life itself.

The story opens with the sterile, artificial quality of the setting made explicit: "Everything (he kept saying) is something it isn't." The names of things were "tex," "koid," "duroid"—all artificial words with no antecedents or roots. Then the central character thinks of the rats in the laboratory, driven insane by being trained to jump at card doors for food, and then the cards would be changed and wouldn't give way any more. The connection between the man and the rats is made when he thinks, "He didn't know which door (or wall) or opening in the house to jump at, to get through . . . There have been so many doors changed on me . . . in the last twenty years" (77-79).

White, having established the ersatz setting of the story, and having identified man's predicament with that of the rats in a laboratory, becomes more specific about that predicament. For the doors, literal to the rats, are symbolic to the man. "First," says the man, "they would teach you the prayers and the Psalms, and that would be the right door . . . and the long sweet words with the holy sound, and that would be the one to jump at to get where the food was." The point is that the "truths" learned aren't permanent; the prayers and the psalms won't always work, and sometime when you jump the door won't give way, "so that all you got was the bump on the nose, and the first bewilderment, the first young bewilderment" (79).

And, for man, the doors will keep on being changed; and man will still jump, for "nobody can not jump." Here man and the rats differ. Then White brings in a touching reference, as Steinhoff has suggested, to Don Marquis. The man says "You wouldn't want me, standing here, to tell you, would you, about my friend the poet (deceased) who said, 'My heart has followed all my days something I cannot name'? . . . And like many poets, although few so beloved, he is gone. It killed him, the jumping" (80).

Another door that man learns after the prayers and the psalms, and it works for a while, is the one "with the picture of the girl on it (only it was spring), her arms outstretched in loveliness . . . ." You would go through the door "winged and exalted (like any rat) and the food would be there . . . and you had chosen the right door for the world was young"(80). There is one cure for man, one ironic hope of escaping the unopening door—to have the prefrontal lobe removed.[3] But then, man will cease to be man; the work of centuries will be removed: "The higher animal becomes a little easier in his mind and more like the lower one"(82).

But the man in the story does not cease being a man, and he achieves a kind of victory at the end: he goes to a door, as he leaves the model home, and faces the risk of a shattering bump. However, the door opens for him— he had half expected to find "one of the old doors . . . the one with the girl her arms outstretched in loveliness and beauty before him." It was not so; still, he gets out, but not quite free, not quite untouched; the symptom of his tension, the projection of his inner turmoil to the world outside, meets him as he steps off the escalator, and "the ground came up slightly, to meet his foot" (82).

As suggested above, the man achieves a kind of victory at the end, for he is still a man; he still keeps jumping. But his is only a partial triumph; the story ends with the final dislocation of the ground when it moves up to meet the foot. The triumph is not one to inspire confidence:

man has been hurt too deeply, too badly, to survive indefinitely the "prefabricated humming," the "mini-piano,"
the "thrutex": all of these are too much. In a life where
man is always confronted "by situations which were in-
capable of being solved," the last try must come. "For
although my heart has followed all my days something
I cannot name, I am tired of jumping and I do not know
which way to go" (81).

Steinhoff, noting that indeed the ground does seem to
come up to meet one's feet when one steps off an escalator,
sees in the end a real victory. The story, he says, "ends
in health": the man "comes back to honest light and to
other people."[4] To the man, though, the end is not a sign
of health but of fear. He had said earlier to himself, "If
only . . . the ground wouldn't come up to meet your
foot the way it does" (79). The story is really one of White's
most pessimistic statements about the human predicament.
The man does go safely through the last door; but in pro-
jecting his growing madness into the world outside the
artificial world of the model house, and in creating a mad
nature where the ground moves up to meet his feet, he is
destroying the one source of hope, the one place to which
he might turn. And this story was written before man
had begun in earnest the business of destroying his en-
vironment: before fall-out, the intensification of air and
water pollution, the uncontrolled use of pesticides.

At the end, the man has achieved not victory, not health,
but the kind of uneasy truce that modern life represented
for White, the kind of uneasy truce that was New York City,
or any large city. We live close to the edge of collapse,
and each day is survived, each jump at each door is made,
with no more hope or confidence for the day to come
than there was for the day just past. As Jane Harrison
puts it: "Each generation has its own terrors; we are now
not panicstricken by the pains of Hell, we shiver instead
before the perils of heredity, the hidden germ, the broken nerve, the insistent *phobia*."[5]

The title story, "The Second Tree from the Corner"
(May 31, 1947), has a clearer structure than "The Door,"
is lighter in tone, and less pessimistic. It opens with Trex-

ler, the main character, in a psychiatrist's office. To the
doctor's question, "Ever have any bizarre thoughts?" he
finally answers defensively, "No." He thinks: "What
kind of thoughts *except* bizarre had he had since the age
of two?"(97). Trexler shows the fear that haunts modern
man when he looks at the titles of the medical books in
the doctor's office and wonders if he has some disease:
"Forty years, he thought, and I still get thrown by the
title of a medical book" (98). (White, we might note, had
often half-humorously imagined himself harboring some
disease). Then, the first shift in  the story comes as Trexler
looks at the doctor and finds *him* looking "rather tired."
The doctor, who says that Trexler is scared, points out
how Trexler has moved his chair away from him. The
doctor here is dominant. As Trexler leaves, he sees in the
office another man, also looking frightened—probably,
thinks Trexler, he has read about heart-disease fatality in
the *Times*. Trexler's visits become routine, with no improvement.

Another and more important shift comes in the story as
Trexler and the doctor begin to merge. First, the doctor
nods his head knowingly when Trexler tells him that he
finds relief in drinking. Then, when Trexler asks the doctor
if he knows what he wants, the doctor's chair moves slightly away from Trexler. "Scared as a rabbit," Trexler says
to himself. "Look at him scoot!" (101). Trexler, however,
does not press his advantage; relaxing again as the patient,
he thinks about the doctor in a new way: "Poor, scared,
overworked bastard" (102). The two are now close together; Trexler's problem is the doctor's problem. They
may not be sure what they want out of life; but, whatever
it is, modern life is not providing it.

At the end, Trexler, while walking one evening, discovers
what it is he wants. "Inexpressible, and unattainable," it
is symbolized by something he sees for a moment: "Suddenly
his sickness seemed health, his dizziness stability. A
small tree, rising between him and the light, stood there
saturated with the evening, each gilt-edged leaf perfectly
drunk with excellence and delicacy . . . . 'I want the
second tree from the corner, just as it stands' " (102).

It is not nature that Trexler, or man wants, but what
nature can symbolize: something "deep, formless, enduring,
and impossible of fulfillment." For the moment, Trexler,
unembarrassed by his fears, is content to be sick (for he is
not "cured"—the disease of modern life is incurable).
The momentary glimpse of truth has given him courage; it
cannot last, but Trexler "crossed Madison, boarded a down-
town bus, and rode all the way to Fifty-second Street
before he had a thought that could rightly have been called
bizarre" (103). The point is basically the same as in "The
Door"—no final solution, no permanent cure, exists for
the disease of life, for the fears it engenders, for the manipulations we must endure. But there is momentary relief, the
tentative victory; and, doctor or patient, the hopeful man
can find it and, like Trexler, glimpse "the flashy tail feathers
of the bird courage" (103).

Two other treatments of this central theme of *The Second
Tree from the Corner,* "The Decline of Sport" (October
25, 1947) and "The Morning of the Day They Did It,"
(February 25, 1950), are amusing fantasies of life in the
future—projections that are not so far out now as they might
have seemed when published. The first concerns the
extremes men will go to in order to achieve simultaneous
presentation of as many athletic events as possible.

The climax of such simultaneous presentations, and the
beginning of the decline of sport, comes in 1975 when a
spectator shoots a football player who has just dropped
a forward pass and muffed the winning touchdown. At the
same moment, the spectator has watched his horse lose a
race being shown on a huge television screen behind the goal
posts; has heard on his radio that his favorite short-stop
had struck out in the last game of the World Series, leaving three men on base; and has seen in the sky-writing
overhead the news that the soccer team on which his son
was playing goalie has lost.

The shot fired by the defeat-tormented spectator sets
off a chain reaction: two sky-writing planes collide and
crash, causing a pileup on a parkway; and panic breaks out
in stadiums all across the country. At the end of that day
of simultaneous presentation of sports, 20,003 persons were

killed. As attendance at these events declined, "even the parkways fell into disuse as motorists rediscovered the charms of old, twisty roads that led through main streets and past barnyards, with their mild congestions and pleasant smells" (45).

As a sketch about the growing complexity and unreality of modern life, not much is missing. A few refinements White may be forgiven for not anticipating are two common practices on television sportcasts: the superimposition on the screen of the scores of other contests while the one being presented is going on, and the "instant replay" gimmick—both techniques that increase the barrier between reality and the viewer.

In "The Morning of the Day They Did It," set in some not-too-distant time in the future, White takes the themes of unreality and complexity a step farther, and throws a few jabs at advertising, literary pretenders, McCarthyism, and the army. Television, we discover, is now being transmitted by plane (earwigs, defeating science, were eating coaxial transmission cables). The story opens on the climactic day when the narrator boards the relay plane and listens to a program called "Author, Please!" starring Melonie Babson, whose book on euthanasia, *Peace of Body*, largely written by someone else, was a best-seller. The program is sponsored by a dress-shield company.

This incident is only the beginning. As the program continues, a doctor assigned to the plane is requested to offer emergency assistance. In a scramble that rivaled in complexity anything that White had written about before, a Diaheliper (providing aerial diaper service to rural areas) collides with a government crop-spraying plane, and the two crash into a whooping-crane sanctuary. Diapers are scattered about, as well as a deadly pesticide, Tri-D—so toxic, incidentally, that everyone as a matter of course has to take preventive shots at regular intervals. This accident is still only a prelude. The narrator takes part in a program, "Town Meeting of the Upper Air," in which a Major General Artemus T. Recoil interviews two army officers stationed six hundred miles up on a space platform equipped with a "liberal supply of the New Weapon," and known as the SPCA (the Space Platform for Checking Aggression). Beyond the pull of gravity, says White, the platform has all the trappings of a great scientific achievement, except that the oxygen on the platform is supplied by large squash vines. The public eagerly awaits news of the magnificent enterprise.

The two officers speak frankly in the interview, refusing to follow the usual inane pattern of such things. To the General's comment that it is "interesting" that there is no weather on the platform, one of them replies, " 'The hell it is . . . It's God-damn dull' " (66). The interview degenerates; when the two officers realize that they are free from the pulls of conscience, as well as gravity, the end is near. They talk, as the world listens:

> "You feel like doing a little shooting, Obie?"
> "You're rootin' tootin' I feel like shootin'."
> "Then what are we waiting for?" (68).

The "New Weapon" destroys the earth, and the narrator finds himself on another planet, with vaguely nostalgic feelings.

As he thinks back about the earth and those last days, he summarizes what was (and is) wrong: "A sort of creeping ineptitude had set in," he says; people were confused, unstable. "There were so many religions in conflict, each ready to save the world with its own dogma, each perfectly intolerant of the other" (69,70). Television, too, had taken its toll: "Children early formed the habit of gaining all their images at second hand, by looking at a screen; they grew up believing that anything perceived directly was vaguely fraudulent" (70). The new planet is pleasant enough: the people are witless and improvident, and thus escape "many of the errors of accomplishment." The apples are wormy but have a wonderful flavor. In fact, the new planet rather resembles earth as it might have been with less "progress," if crops had not been sprayed, if there had been less ambition or fewer urgencies in life.

Now it has been impossible to include in this summary all the points in the story, which is twice as long as any other in the collection. As White's most elaborate comment on contemporary life, it lacks the subtlety and sensitivity of "The Door," or "The Second Tree from the Corner," and is artistically inferior to these two. Yet it nonetheless sums up a good part of what White had to say about life in the post-World War II world. The story takes place in a brave new world where everything is provided by the government, including a "babysitz fund," but where the zest for living has gone; the narrator's wife mournfully wishes she might live dangerously and be able to buy some flowers. The United States is marked by a perversion of good taste, by good intentions and evil actions, and by the disappearance of decent cultural values. The program is sponsored by a dress-shield company; the space platform is ironically called the SPCA; and the world federalists have become impotent in the face of a dimly disguised Daughters of the American Revolution. Birds have disappeared, pesticides are so powerful that the people take protective shots, and the complex life is daily on the verge of calamity.

As in the case of his other projections into the future, White can be forgiven for not being a perfect prophet. He wrote his story before Rachel Carson's *Silent Spring;* we have cluttered space with far more debris than he could have imagined; and, if he had intended to suggest lack of taste by having a dress-shield company the sponsor, no one can blame him for not foreseeing the tastelessness, the grossness, that television advertising could descend to when it really tried.

The final irony in the destruction of the earth by the United States is the narrator's conviction that the country was well-intentioned: "Even I, at this date and at this distance, cannot forget my country's great heart and matchless ingenuity. I can't in honesty say that I believe we were wrong to send the men to the platform—it's just that in any matter involving love, or high explosives, one can never foresee all the factors. . . . It was inevitable that what happened, at last, was conceived in good will" (69).

White's words, of course, have a sharper irony today than they had in 1950. But that this is true suggests that White was essentially right in his analysis of American life and in his prophetic sense about the direction in which we seem to be drifting. Our sense of reality *has* become dimmed—the children in the story, brought up to reject the reality of anything not touched by electronics, have now grown up; and they are the ones who watch crimes in the street unconcerned and who cannot distinguish between the phony violence of the television or movie screen on the one hand, and napalm-inflicted agony on the other.

## IV  *Some Final Items*

Some other pieces in *The Second Tree from the Corner* remain to be considered: a few of the poems, White's parody of Hemingway's *Across the River and into the Trees,* and an endearing little gem, "Death of a Pig." The last, in spite of its subject, death, serves as a healthy and pleasant antidote to White's somewhat gloomy view of the future of urban man under the uncertain hand of science. At the opening of "Death of a Pig," White describes the "antique pattern" of buying a spring pig, feeding it, and killing it at the beginning of winter: "It is a tragedy enacted on most farms with perfect fidelity to the original script" (243). It is also, White implies throughout, an honest ritual with roots deep in the past, and none of the cellophane trappings of, let's say, a town meeting of the upper air.

With a technique he has often used, White summarizes the events first—his pig's taking sick, the attempted cure, the death—and then turns back and relates the whole matter in more leisurely detail. Several times White connects the pig's failing health with half-humorous references to his own feeling of deterioration and to his sense of the transitory, insecure quality of life. A typical touch, the lightly hinted melancholy nicely balances the rising spirits of Fred, White's dachshund, whose gleeful and ghoulish presence provides a unifying and contrasting motif.

White, and then a veterinarian, try to save the ailing pig; when it finally dies, White remarks about the simple decency of the death and burial: there was "no stopover in the undertaker's foul parlor" (252). He returns to the ritualistic symbolism of the opening by noting the solicitude

of the neighbors: "The premature expiration of a pig is
. . . a departure which the  community marks solemnly on
its calendar, a sorrow in which it feels fully involved" (253).

The sketch, neither profound nor wholly serious, presents effectively the confrontation of life and death, and
the ironic shift as White the farmer-butcher becomes
suddenly the physician and the consoler of his pig. It
is ironic too that death in the traditional rural setting can
have a dignity that is hard to find elsewhere today. Only
in a rural setting, probably, could one be involved so
clearly and so simply with the honest and unadorned
realities of life, and only in this setting could White
show so well, and without affectation, that death, even
the death of a pig, is not routine.

In "Across the Street and into the Grill," one of his
best spoofs, White parodies Hemingway's novel *Across
the River and into the Trees*. White chose his subject well;
the novel, probably Hemingway's worst, deserves parody.
White, I am sure, would grant that Hemingway's style at
its best is beyond parody, but in a style like Hemingway's
there is a thin dividing line between effectiveness and
affectation—like the thin line between sentiment and
sentimentality in much of Charles Dickens.

One of the functions of the parodist is to discover these
fine lines and, by crossing them, to show the  dangers and
vulnerability of the style. With devastating skill White
does precisely this, concentrating on chapters XI and XII
of Hemingway's novel. His technique is to select certain
words and phrases Hemingway used; placing them in a
slightly different context, he pinpoints the foolishness of
the original. This method can best be illustrated by citing
parallel passages.

Hemingway:    "They kissed for a long time, standing straight
              and kissing true."
White:        "She stepped into a phone booth and dialled
              true and well, using her finger."
Hemingway:    [the scene where the Colonel operates the ele-
              vator]: "'We can run it ourselves . . . I checked

out on elevators long ago.' It was a good ride with a slight bump, and a rectification at the end."

White:    "In the elevator, Perley took the controls. 'I'll run it,' he said to the operator. 'I checked out long ago.' He stopped true at the third floor."

Still, it is not in the specific word echoes that the greatest success of "Across the Street and into the Grill" lies, but rather in White's dead-pan parody of the fatuous, trivial tone of the whole scene in the novel. It is the posed and phony heroism, the pseudo-realistic, irrelevant details, that White singles out for ridicule. For example, there is something contrived and untrue when the Colonel and the "Gran Maestro" reminisce about the past and each asks the other if he remembers certain events: " 'And we would throw the empty fiascos [White had his characters going to Schraffts, where "they have the mayonnaise in fiascos" (140)] at the station guards from the troop trains.' " And: " 'We would throw all the left-over grenades away and bounce them down the hillside coming back from the Grappa.' " This passage cries for the parody that White provides: " 'Boticelli, do you remember when we took all the mailing envelopes from the stock room, spit on the flaps, and then drank rubber cement till the foot-soldiers arrived?' " (142).

White was not unfair in his take-off. In fact, there are sections of the novel where Hemingway almost seems to be parodying himself. For example, after the girl and the Colonel kiss, "true, in the cold of the open windows," this follows: " 'Oh,' she said. Then, 'Oh.' " A parodist need do no more with this than to let it stand untouched.

There are twelve poems in all in *The Second Tree from the Corner*. Nine of these are in a special section, "Nine Songs"; two are book reviews in poetic form; and one, "Zoo Revisited," was published here for the first time. In general the poems, dating mostly from the late 1940's, lack either the lyrical or the satirical quality of the best of White's earlier poetry. Two, in addition to "Zoo Revisited," stand above the rest; "The Red Cow Is Dead," and "Song of the Queen Bee" show well White's amusing and felicitous use of contemporary news items. The "Song of the Queen Bee," for example, got its start from a Department of Agriculture bulletin on artificial insemination in bee breeding; it is a pleasant expression of the freedom of a life that refuses to be mechanized. The difficulty in bee breeding comes from the queen bee's habit of mating in the air "with whatever drone she encounters." This quotation from the Department of Agriculture gives White the refrain for his poem:

> And it's simply rare
> In the upper air,
>     And I wish to state
>     That I'll *always* mate
> With whatever drone I encounter.

"Zoo Revisited, Or the Life and Death of Olie Hackstaff," is White's most complicated poem; the E. B. White collection at Cornell contains over seventy pages of notes and preliminary versions. The poem was not published until *The Second Tree from the Corner,* but clearly White had been thinking about it for quite some time previous to its publication: included among the notes for the poem is a clipping about traffic fatalities from *The New York Times* of November 8, 1937.

In six parts in a variety of styles, the poem has a theme similar to that of "Once More to the Lake"—the duality between past and present, youth and age, father and son. If the name "Hackstaff" has a significance, it escapes me. It may be a play on "Shakespeare," but I doubt it. White, in his notes, had considered other names—"Schoolboy Mosley," and "Schoolboy Colfax," for example, and in a letter he writes, "As far as I know, the name Olie Hackstaff is simply an invention of mine. I needed a name."[6]

Part I describes a visit to the zoo by Olie Hackstaff and his son; they look at a bison, and Mr. Hackstaff thinks back to his youth:

> Here stands the bull Myself, alone, with his
>     torrential need,

> At home with living death, at rest with reservoirs
>    of seed;
> Pause here my self, my soul, my son, by this
>    encrusted rail. . . .

*Don't put your mouth on that dirty old rail!*

This last line, the kind of thing a parent or nurse would say to a child, makes the  transition to Part II, where Mr. Hackstaff returns fully to his past. As White puts it in one of his manuscript notes, "Standing in front of the bars reminds Mr. Hackstaff of moments associated with a backyard zoo he used to pass on his way home from school at the end of the morning. He sees himself in a flash the small boy Olie sitting in his fourth grade class, with his fear of the basement." In this part, Mr. Hackstaff recalls first his anguished waiting for school to be over so he can go to the bathroom ("I can't wait./I have to go."), and  then his puzzlement over sex ("Why does an older boy like Kenny/Laugh when he tells the rabbit's story?").

Part III describes Mr. Hackstaff's taking his son and wife to a resort hotel where he recalls another aspect of his youth — his sense of well-being after swimming, and at the same time his curious sense  of unfulfillment that the holiday produces ("How well I know this sultry scene/where dreaming summer takes her toll/her cruel toll"). In Part IV, Mr. Hackstaff, still reliving his youth, recalls making a toy sword and thinking about the unsettling question of war. But, instead of answers to the question, Part IV ends with a series of platitudinous parental admonitions—"keep your feet dry/don't take cold"—and is followed by Part V, a short section on still another recollection, adolescent love: "It is in youth there comes, and one time only,/This dream of love, this flowerform of light."

The last part of the poem, "The Hospital," recapitulates the earlier sections and concludes with the death, presumably, of Mr. Hackstaff. In a delirium, he recalls fragments of his youth: the zoo and the bull, his curiosity about reproduction, the fragments of good advice from adults, and love. The poem ends with a touch of melodrama as an announcement comes over the  hospital intercom: "Dr.

Ternidad! Dr. Breese!" indicating, we assume, the last moments of Mr. Hackstaff.

This summary suggests, I hope, White's main intention—to show through the identity of father and son the duality, the simultaneity, of human experience; the tentative nature of that experience; and the circular quality of time. The poem is a combination, in a way, of "Once More to the Lake" and "The Door," except that, instead of stopping with the premonition or anticipation of death, it proceeds to the final moment. The manuscript notes make clear, if the poem itself does not, its autobiographical elements.

In the first part, we are reminded on the literal level of White's own love of zoos; on another level, the bison suggests desire, creativity ("The seminal imperative"), qualities that were part of White's childhood when even then he had felt the drive to be a writer. In Part II, Mr. Hackstaff recalls his reluctance to use the school bathroom and his curiosity about how rabbits reproduce. Part of this is certainly autobiographical: one of White's school friends had a backyard zoo, very likely including a rabbit hutch. In the poem, the boy's name is Whipple; in one of the manuscript notes, the name is Mendel; and, in a frankly autobiographical sketch in *The New Yorker* ("Was Lifted by Ears as a Boy, No Harm Done," May 9, 1964), White mentions the Mendels as one of the families in his neighborhood. At any rate, Part II marks the progress of a young boy into adolescence.

This progress continues in Part III, "By the Sea," and the autobiographical elements appear strong here also. White's fondness for the sea is well enough known, and one of his notes suggests that he intended the sea to be symbolic: "The sea is the mother of trouble, sponsor of ill./Smelling of now and forever." Another and longer note again implies that the poem is partly about White, and it also reinforces the interpretation of the poem that has been given so far:

The wind, and how its sound went so far back into time, blowing before life, before his life, before anybody's life, would be blowing

after his death, after everyone's death. Adelaide, sure he was
not going to marry her, too predictable, but the dances in the
casino, the sailing, windblownness, wet and spray everywhere,
sands and the sunburn and combing his hair with sand in comb
and hair all pointing up toward: war, school, earning living,
sex expression, marriage.

The next two parts, IV and V, continue with Mr. Hackstaff's
recollection of his maturing. The two parts involve questions
of war and love—two problems, certainly, in White's
mind as he was finishing high school and wondering what
to do—go off to college or join the army. In a note on this
part of the poem, White asks, "What were the questions
in those days? Life, love, war, girls . . . "And, finally, in
another note, the problems reappear: " . . . uncertainty
about war, and whether to go back to school or war, enormous vitality and vitalness of life at that time, all heading
toward pointing toward pointing at getting on toward
SOMETHING, some point, some thing . . . ."
We can read this poem as one more statement of White's
early sense of purpose, his drive, and at the same time his
bewilderment over particular goals, his gnawing sense
of failure; conflicts that did not come to an end until his
employment by *The New Yorker* and his marriage. And
just as Mr. Hackstaff saw his own past through his son, so
White at times saw his own past through his son Joel (some
of the notes to "Zoo Revisited," in particular a short poem
not included in the final version, contain references to
"Joe").
The idea of the circularity of time is connected with
White's feeling of the imminence of death. From father
to son and back to father again, and this time the son
as the new and replacing father: this circularity is the central theme of "Once More to the Lake," and of this poem.
It may be at the center of White's belief, or philosophy,
if so formal a word can be used for what he has never
been very formal about. In "The Ring of Time," in *Points
of My Compass*, White gives an explicit statement of
that belief, which is partly an illusion. For time, not

really circular, moves always away from a point, and it is one of the comforting and necessary elements of faith that experiences can be recaptured, that the best moments will return. As will be seen in Chapter VIII, the structure of *The Points of My Compass*, ending as it does with White's retrospective "The Years of Wonder," suggests the idea of circularity; at the same time it shows the inevitable loss of the past and of man's dreams.

Finally, and this is one of the virtues of the poem, Mr. Hackstaff's experience, and White's, is that of many sensitive, thinking people. White could put this universal experience in simple and honest terms. It may be true that some adolescents in White's day, or today, make their discoveries of sex in precocious and sensational ways, ways some growing-up novels describe in rich detail. But it may also be true that a good many others grow up like E. B. White, and wonder, as Mr. Hackstaff wondered as a boy:

> Why does an older boy like Kenny
> Laugh when he tells the rabbit's story?
> Why does he hang around the hutch
> Where something happens that you have to know—
> Something the buck does with the doe,
> Something that's sad and terrible to know?
> (Everybody has to know.)
>
> ("Zoo Revisited," Part II)

## CHAPTER 8

## "The Ring of Time"

*T*HE *Points of My Compass* (1962), the last published collection of White's work, includes material written from the summer of 1954 to March 1961. White has published relatively little since, and the collection contains his most personal and explicit statements on a number of matters; it also contains some of his best essays.

During the period covered by *The Points of My Compass* White continued to write for "Notes and Comment," though on an increasingly reduced scale until, by 1960, he was contributing just a few items a year. He continued to write the tag-lines for the newsbreaks department, published a number of poems and sketches that have not yet been reprinted, and brought out in 1959 a revised edition of William Strunk's *The Elements of Style,* to which he added an introduction and a chapter about writing.

And some mention should be made of a project White and his wife had thought of—a book about *The New Yorker.* The two had accumulated a large number of letters and notes (now a part of the E. B. White collection at Cornell), and it is to be regretted that the project was never completed. Since White and his wife had been with *The New Yorker* almost from the start, they knew as much about it as anyone. The project may have been abandoned because the scope of the work dismayed White; he has not found long or sustained writing congenial. He may also have felt the difficulty of presenting adequately the portrait of

Ross, for whom he had great affection. Finally, White and his wife may have been reluctant to add to *The New Yorker* story and to the Ross legend after Kramer's *Ross and The New Yorker* (1951), and especially after Thurber's *The Years with Ross* (1959), although the Whites could undoubtedly have contributed much new material.

The essays in *The Points of My Compass* fall into what are now familiar patterns for White: national and international affairs, the idea of progress, the urban and rural scenes and, in two notable essays, the circularity of time—a theme in much of White's writing and one present by implication in a number of these last essays. In fact, the whole collection, ending as it does with an autobiographical essay that goes back to White's days in Seattle and Alaska, suggests the idea of circularity. Also, to many of these essays White has written postscripts containing "afterthoughts and later information." They add to the feeling of circularity.

We find also a curious sort of geographical circularity in the collection. Though White had returned to permanent residence at his farm in Maine in 1957, he made occasional visits elsewhere, and the essays are datelined from the four points of the compass, depending on what direction from *The New Yorker* office in Manhattan he happened to be when he wrote them. This "geographical distortion," as he calls it, seems to broaden the dimensions of the work; but it also underlines the importance of New York City to White. It was for him a microcosm, a center, and the four corners of the world could almost be contained within its emotional if not geographical limits. Geography *was* to White something of an emotional matter; it is, he says, "undergoing vast shifts anyway, with populations in turmoil and the weathercock spinning wildly as the wind veers" (xiii). Without being pompous about it, we could say that the essays represent the culmination of White's experience, the farthest point of navigation—not quite to the heart of darkness, perhaps, but certainly to the heart of his message to his readers.

I  *Politics, National and International*

A good part of White's message has to do with politics, national and international; in four essays—"Bedfellows," "Sootfall and Fallout," "The Shape of the U. N.," and "Unity"—he presents what are at this date (1973) his final thoughts on the subject. "Bedfellows" (February 6, 1956), more political than any other of White's essays, concerns McCarthyism and orthodoxy. It proceeds, in a manner characteristic of White, with a theme and counterpoint —the counterpoint in this case being once again White's dachshund, Fred. Fred, an exaggerator and zealot, is an investigator who sees a security risk in every bird and squirrel. White had been reminded of this disposition of Fred by a quotation from Justice Brandeis, who had said that the greatest dangers to liberty "lurk in insidious encroachment by men of zeal, well-meaning but without understanding" (40).

White disliked loyalty investigations and he was also disturbed by a statement of President Eisenhower implying that religious faith was a part of the American way of life. On the contrary, White says, America should never "become an uncomfortable place for the unbeliever . . . . Democracy is itself a religious faith. . . . When I see the first faint shadow of orthodoxy sweep across the sky . . . I tremble all over." White had never tried to apply a label to himself; his discomfort with orthodoxy was obvious, and he shares the discomfort with his wife, who comments after President Eisenhower's appeal to Americans to pray: "For the first time in my life I'm beginning to feel like an outsider in my own land" (46).

In the postscript to the essay, written six years later, White, speaking of the Birch society, is pleased that it has not been able to get the same headlines McCarthy did. He also comments approvingly about the recent Supreme Court decision on prayers in school: "From the violence of the reaction you would have thought the Court was in the business of stifling America's religious life and that the country was going to the dogs. But I think the Court

again heard clearly the simple theme that ennobles our
Constitution: that no one shall be made to feel uncomfortable or unsafe because of noncomformity" (48).

In the next three essays, those dealing with the international scene, White writes on one of his favorite themes,
world unity, repeating some of what he said in *The Wild
Flag*—the desperate need for some machinery to recognize
and enforce the interdependence of nations. Much had
happened since 1945, and he was intensely aware of the
problems brought about by the hydrogen bomb, especially
the atmospheric pollution from atomic testing, and the
problem of arms control. In "Sootfall and Fallout" (Oct.
18, 1956—date of composition, not publication), White
makes two observations: the H-bomb has muddied the
concept of "freedom through strength"; for, although
it may be a deterrent of war, "it has little virtue as a *weapon*
of war" (82). Second, atomic testing has produced a problem "that is clearly a community problem, devoid of
nationality—the problem of the total pollution of the
planet" (85). In his discussion, White touches on a problem, not yet sufficiently debated, that the Viet Nam conflict has made vivid: the atom, he notes, has "altered the
concept of personal sacrifice for moral principle. . . . I
doubt whether any noble principle—or any ignoble
principle, either, for that matter—can be preserved at
the price of genetic disintegration" (82).

The real problem, of course, is the absence of a new
concept of international order to match the new science
of destruction. White sees a few encouraging examples of
international     cooperation,     "little     pockets     of     unity,"
like the developing European common market, or the United
Nations International Children's Emergency Fund. The
United Nations itself, however, was not a new form: "In
its structure . . . [it] reaffirms everything that caused
World    War    II";    it    is    "modern    in    intent,    old-
fashioned in *shape*." White had not really revised his
attitude toward the United Nations; but, in the ten years
or so of its operation since *The Wild Flag*, the organization had revealed about as many weaknesses as strengths—it
had failed in Hungary, for example, but had been success-

ful in the Suez crisis of 1956—and some of his enthusiasm had disappeared. In "The Shape of the U.N." (December 1, 1956) White writes retrospectively about the Preamble and Chapter One of the United Nations Charter.

To White the stylist, the wording of the Charter is weak, particularly in its condemnation of "aggression," an undefinable word. Each member of the United Nations will interpret the word in his own way; in the first place, to define "aggression," "it is necessary to get into the realm of right and wrong, and the Charter of the United Nations studiously avoids this delicate area" (96). In the second place, "to condemn aggression is to decide *in advance of an event* the merits of the dispute" (97). (The manipulations of the word by both sides, or all sides, in the Viet Nam conflict show how prophetic White was.)

Another weakness White saw in the United Nations was its failure to lay down rules of conduct for its members. Since its beginning, White wrote, "almost everything that has happened indicates that the United Nations should never have admitted the Communist nations on *their* terms; that is, freedom to operate behind a wall" (95). To White, the United Nations, "the shaky shape of the world's desire for order" (99), is better than nothing; but to *establish* that order it must do more.

In a postscript to the essay, written six years later, White cites the Indian invasion of Goa as a perfect example of the problem of defining "aggression." He also expresses skepticism about "strengthening" the United Nations "not in the hope of its becoming a government but with the intention of improving its services." To this comment White adds five specific recommendations:

1. A nation that jams the air shall not be eligible for membership.
2. A member of the U.N. that jams the air shall be expelled.
3. A nation that builds a wall to prevent people from leaving the country shall not be eligible for membership.
4. In the case of members whose press is run by the government, the privilege of using the forum shall carry with it the obligation to report fully the proceedings of the forum, in the home press. . . .

5. Member states shall grant the Secretary General and his aides free access to the country at all times (102).

These interesting suggestions reveal well the common-sense approach of White to foreign affairs—and they reveal at the same time a certain innocence about them. For one thing, the recommendations are a mixture of general propositions, and contain at least one proposal that is specifically directed toward the Berlin wall. White might suggest taking the term "wall" metaphorically, but to do so would immediately create the same problem of definition he had noted with regard to "aggression." It could also be argued whether the terms "report fully," "free access," and even "jamming" can be clearly defined. Still, the same comment can be made here as in my chapter on *The Wild Flag*: what White probably hoped was not so much to see his recommendations literally adopted but to create a climate of opinion, an attitude, without which no international organization of any sort could operate successfully.

White elaborates tangentially on this matter of climate of opinion in his next essay on foreign affairs, "Unity," (June 1960). Writing shortly after the U-2 incident and the suddenly cancelled Paris summit meeting, he discusses, among other matters, the subject of disarmament, opposing the general view that disarmament is the key to peace. The truth, he says, is that arms are the symptom, not the cause, of war; the answer is not the control of weapons, "but the creation of machinery for the solution of the problems that give rise to the use of weapons" (179). He implies that, with the right climate of opinion, disarmament would cease to be the issue.

In short, some political means must be found to make war unnecessary. For one thing, White feels that disarmament is a device "by which a nation tries to increase its strength relative to the strength of others" (179). For another thing, he notes that inspection of arms would be difficult; it would tend to increase secrecy among nations, and an enforcement agency could not work so long as there was no authority "higher and more powerful than that of the parties involved in the deal" (182).

What was needed—and here White departs from his earlier hopes of the United Nations—is the bringing together of free men "in a political community and under a common roof." The Communists, he adds, are already united in the pursuit of their common goal of communizing the world, but the West lacks a common purpose. If the Western democracies could "act in a united and constructive way," if there could emerge a "federal union of free democratic capitalist states," there would be some hope of united action and of the elimination not merely of arms but of the need of war. White hopes that a federal union such as he envisages will ultimately comprise most of the nations of the world.

White recognizes that the very existence of arms creates a state of tension, but he suggests that the absence of arms might create even greater tensions: "An arms race is a frightening thing, but eighty sovereign nations suddenly turning up without arms is truly terrifying" (183). He also acknowledges a distinction between nuclear and conventional arms, and grants that a test-ban treaty makes sense because nuclear testing produced a threat to all nations, including the nation doing the testing: "national self-interest happens in this case to coincide with universal interest." Our hope, White concludes, lies in Western unity; he quotes with enthusiastic approval a statement by Salvador de Madariaga: " 'The trouble today . . . is that the Communist world understands unity but not liberty, while the free world understands liberty but not unity. Eventual victory may be won by the first of the two sides to achieve the synthesis of both liberty and unity' " (188).

Since this essay represents one of White's last published statements about international affairs and world government, it deserves attention. White, as we have noted, has moved away from the hope for the United Nations that he had had when he wrote *The Wild Flag* essays; two things in particular made him change his views: events had shown painfully the weaknesses of the United Nations Charter

and of the United Nations itself; and the proliferation
of nuclear arms had introduced a complicating and frightening element into the world scene.

The problem of disarmament is immensely complicated
— the Geneva Conference on Disarmament has been in
session, off and on, since the mid-1950's. White, approaching
the problem with humility, has perhaps missed something:
granted, arms are at the beginning an *effect*, not the *cause*
of a problem. Still, effects, like means, have a way of shifting: arms tend to beget arms, and the existence of power
almost inevitably leads to an exercise of it. Surely the re-
duction or limitation of arms can have a good psychological
effect that can lead to a relaxation of tension and help produce an atmosphere conducive to discussions of the *real*
problems.

Furthermore, and this is a major challenge to White's thesis,
the problem of world unity simply cannot be regarded in
terms of "free" Western democracies versus the Communist
bloc. The Communist states were not so united in 1960
as White implies, and since 1960 the lack of solidarity
has become more apparent. A union of capitalist democracies might be a good idea (but why *capitalist*? What about
the Scandinavian countries?). Such a union, however,
would not, *ipso facto*, create a world comprised of the forces
of freedom and those of Communism. Where, in addition to the Scandinavian countries, would be nations
like India, Pakistan, Israel, the Arab nations, or the emerging African countries? Democracy and capitalism sometimes seem in developing nations to be irrelevant con-
cepts, nor do they lend themselves to easy definition.

Perhaps the greatest weakness in White's argument is his
assumption of virtue on the part of the West, though in
fairness to White, we must admit that such assumptions
were easier to hold in 1960 than now. "The West," he
writes, "has a real genius for doing approximately what the
East wants it to do. . . . I am beginning to tire of running
the East's errands and dropping into the East's traps, and
I wish I could set off on a different journey, under good
auspices" (175-76). We set off on a different journey in
Viet Nam, but the experience, to say the least, has made

us wary of asserting our virtue, although we may well have fallen into a trap.

One more objection is that White has asserted that an argument against disarmament without a supranational political authority is that nuclear weapons were a deterrent to war. Unusable weapons, he says, "stand poised and quiet . . . . If modern weapons make war unlikely, had we not better keep them until we have found the political means of making war unnecessary?" Unfortunately, events since 1960 have made it painfully clear that, in spite of the supposed deterrent effect of nuclear weapons, a large-scale war with conventional weapons is still very much possible.

In spite of all these objections, White's essay makes sense. Disarmament *is* a means to an end, and White is right in warning that we should not confuse the symptom with a basic disorder. He is also right in stating the need for a world political organization. And, if his ideas about a union of Western democracies to oppose what he took to be a monolithic Communist force are open to objections, the main point of "Unity" remains valid: the world *does* need "Something Good Happening." "What is this good thing?" he asks. "I think it is the evolution of community, community slowly and surely invested with the robes of government by the consent of the governed. We cannot conceivably achieve a peaceful life merely by relaxing the tensions of sovereign nations; there is an unending supply of them" (178).

## II *"Progress"*

Just as these essays we have discussed are among White's latest statements in international affairs, so others round off his ideas about progress and the dilemma of modern man. It is likely, however, that these comments, in essay form, will seem to some readers less effective than the imaginative sketches and stories in *The Second Tree from the Corner*. In one of these essays, "A Slight Sound at Evening," written in the summer of 1954, White pays a centenary tribute to Thoreau. Whether he had read Thoreau

in college and how much his views have been shaped by
Thoreau are questions that have been touched on in Chapter III. It seems clear that White's real interest in Thoreau began in 1927, when he bought a World's Classics
edition of *Walden.* "Since then," he says, "I have carried
it about with me on the cars and in buses and boats, as it is the
most amusing detective story I possess" *(The Second Tree
from the Corner,* 94). The essay from which the above quotation is taken accounts humorously for the way Thoreau's
words tend to creep into White's conversation. The present essay, a more serious discussion, summarizes White's
feelings about Thoreau, and considers the relevance of
Thoreau to modern man.

We should read *Walden,* White says, at an age "when
the normal anxieties and enthusiasm and rebellions of
youth closely resemble those of Thoreau in that spring
of 1845, when he borrowed an ax, went out to the woods,
and began to whack down some trees for timber. Received at such a juncture, the book is like an invitation to
life's dance" (15). White himself had discovered Thoreau
at such a time, and he quotes a critical sentence from
*Walden:* " 'I learned this at least by my experiment: that
if one advances confidently in the direction of his dreams,
and endeavors to live the life which he has imagined, he
will meet with a success unexpected in common hours.' "
Then White adds: "The sentence has the power to resuscitate
the youth drowning in his sea of doubt. I recall my exhilaration upon reading it, many years ago, in a time of hesitation
and despair" (17).

In another passage, the relevance of Thoreau to White
is equally clear. To Thoreau's comment that, at a certain
time of life, " 'we are accustomed to consider every spot
as the possible site of a house,' " he replies, "There spoke
the young man, a few years out of college, who had not yet
broken away from home. He hadn't married, and he had
found no job that measured up to his rigid standards of
employment, and like any young man, or young animal,
he felt uneasy and on the defensive until he had fixed
himself a den" (21). White might have been describing himself here.

The essay is interesting for what it reveals of White's state of mind as a young man; it is more interesting for what it says about the importance of Thoreau to others. White concludes that Thoreau was at once the companion and the chider (the "hair-shirt") of the "fellows who hate compromise and have compromised, fellows who love wildness and have lived tamely"; he was the man "who long ago gave corroboration to impulses they perceived were right and issued warnings against things they instinctively knew to be their enemies" (25).

This conclusion, resembling Matthew Arnold's tribute to Ralph Waldo Emerson as the friend of those who live by the spirit, is at the core of White's feeling about modern life. Man does not want to live in a culture filled with gadgets and the "multiplicity of convenience"; he wants to live simply and naturally, but not in primitiveness or barbarity—for White was never ready to surrender all progress, all conveniences. Men should live so as to escape the charge that Thoreau once made when, in a passage White quoted, he describes a farmer fixing a hay baler: " 'This farmer is endeavoring to solve the problem of a livelihood by a formula more complicated than the problem itself.' " White states the matter somewhat differently in a recent piece in *The New York Times* (September 23, 1967), but the conclusion is the same. Expressing half-humorous, half-serious concern about the proliferation of numbers involved in his use of bank checks, White comments: "I'm against machines only when the convenience they afford to some people is regarded as more important than the inconvenience they cause to all."

Two essays in which White faces the question of progress more directly are "The Motorcar" (March 16, 1958), and "The Railroad" (January 28, 1960). In the first, White belabors the auto industry for its styling: the cars look, he says, as if they had been given their final licks "by a group of emotionally disturbed children" (142). The auto industry, he continues, has become so preoccupied with motivational research, with its vision of automobiles as strato-cruisers and rockets, that the basic function of a car—to provide transportation—has been forgotten.

Progress has claimed another victim.

Not so formal an indictment as the summary might suggest, the essay is built around White's frustrated efforts to replace his aging 1949 DeSoto with a new car of equal comfort and headroom. The tone is generally light and ironic, but White ended with a serious comment: "The motorcar is a killer and will always be a killer, but the death rate will always respond to responsible work at the drawing board" (151).

Of course, 1958 was the year when auto design had about reached the ultimate in absurdity: fins and chromium were excessive, headlights were set at crazy angles, and color combinations were grotesque. By 1960, as White noted in a postscript to his essay, styles had changed for the better; it was possible to buy a moderately sane car. But only moderately, for once again White proved to be ahead of the times: he had anticipated Rachel Carson with his fear of insecticides in "The Morning of the Day They Did It"; it was eight years after "The Motorcar" that the problem of safety became enough of an issue to affect the car manufacturers in any meaningful way—and even then government prodding was required to produce "more responsible work at the drawing board."

"The Railroad," one of the longest essays in *The Points of My Compass,* is a plea for the continuation of passenger service, specifically on the Maine Railroads. But beyond that, White speaks of his own personal relationship with the railroad: "I have to admit that it means a great deal to me. . . . It is the link with my past, for one thing, and with the city, for another—two connections I would not like to see broken" (155). Thus baldly stated are two motifs that run through White's work—the past and the contrast between city and country. The essay opens and closes with references to Thoreau, who lived, White says, "in the morningtime of America's railroads." In contrast, White gloomily observes that he himself lives "in the twilight of railroading, the going down of its sun" (156). On the snowy morning White was writing, the roads were a mix of "snow, ice, sand, salt, and trouble"; the airlines had suffered a rash of disasters; and the railroad had abandoned

him. After recalling Thoreau's words about an earlier snowy
day, describing the arrival, despite the weather, of the passenger train to his village, White marks the contrast: "How
different my village from his village, my century from his
century!" (157).

White plays frequently on the ironic contrast between
past and present, between his day and Thoreau's. Midway
in the essay he quotes Thoreau's words that " 'one well-
conducted institution [the railroad] regulates a whole country' "; he concludes the essay with the hope that the passenger trains will not disappear in his own lifetime, for "one
well-conducted institution may still regulate a whole
country" (170). The greatness of the railroads in the past
cannot be denied; to White, that past may be one of their
problems. They are addicted to the past, and their tradi-
tionalism has brought them to their present predicament;
their motto, he suggests, is "What has always been shall
always be" (159).

White nostalgically recalls his first train ride to Maine
in 1905 when his family left the city and traveled to one
of the Belgrade lakes for August (again, we note the link
with the past, and with the city). What strikes him most as he
thinks back is that in 1905 the average speed by train from
New York to Bangor was thirty-one miles an hour; fifty-five
years later it is thirty-four miles an hour. "This is an impressive record," he says; "It's not every institution that
can hold to an ideal through fifty-five years of our fast-
est-moving century. It's not every traveler who is content
to go thirty-four, either" (162). The deterioration in service
continued; in the postscript to the essay, written three
years later, White notes that the average speed from New
York to Bangor had dropped to twenty-eight miles an
hour!

A few hopeful signs exist, however: the ability of trains
to go in weather that would stop planes and buses, and
growing highway congestion that makes automobile travel
more difficult. The trains need government aid, White
grants, but they also need something else: "Railroading
in America enjoyed its monopoly status much too long
for its own good, and the characteristic American genius

for new shapes, new ideas, new ways to exploit demand, although it infects every other business, has been lacking in railroading" (173).

White was far from being alone in mourning the passing of the passenger trains, nor was his concern entirely in terms of nostalgic memories. He writes of the difficulty of taking his sick wife to the hospital by car when no trains were available, and when she was in no condition to be driven. Even today, when transportation problems are much greater than when White wrote, only sporadic attempts have been made to reinstate or improve passenger service; Amtrak has been half-hearted at best.

White's skepticism about progress is clear, and what he has said in these and in some other essays in *The Points of My Compass* has only reinforced what he has said earlier. Our society has become increasingly complex, increasingly technological; and, while complexity has brought improvement in many areas, it has been, to say the least, a mixed blessing. In transportation, in radio, and in television, the losses outweigh the gains. White points out that in television, for example, advertising has obtained the upper hand; the performer has become pitchman because of the practice of having individual advertisers sponsor particular programs: "There is hardly a person of any note in the TV world who does not lead a double life; right in the middle of whatever he is saying or doing, there comes a pause, and the performer holds up a can of cleaning fluid and recites the lesson" (202). The choice of advertising that a newspaper reader has does not exist in television: "The old clarity simply isn't there any more" (203).

The owner of an automobile also has less choice than he ought to have, for in many places he no longer has the option of traveling by train. There are still conveniences in our society, and man can still be an individual, but the task is more difficult than it should be. "I still live fairly high on the hog," White writes, "but it takes an unfaltering spirit of retrogression to accomplish it. The minute I follow the crowd, my standard of living goes down" (197). Little has happened since he wrote this that would alter his opinion. The urban snarls, the conditions approaching anarchy

in some cities, blackouts, air and water pollution; all of
these take us back to the quotation from Thoreau—the
formula is "more complicated than the problem itself"
—and to what may stand as White's clearest statement of
all:

Many of the commonest assumptions, it seems to me, are arbi-
trary ones: that the new is better than the old, the untried superior
to the tried, the complex more advantageous than the simple, the
fast quicker than the slow, the big greater than the small, and
the world as remodelled by Man the Architect functionally
sounder and more agreeable than the world as it was before he
changed everything to suit his vogues and his conniptions. (68-69)

### III *Nature: City and Country*

That quotation was not from an essay about trains, automobiles, or television; it was from "Coon Tree" (July 14,
1956), a rambling account of coons and other things that
introduces another sub-division of *The Points of My
Compass*—essays about nature. In general, these essays
reveal little new about White's interest in the external
world, an interest well recorded in *One Man's Meat*. "The
Rock Dove," however, is an exception; and it can stand as
the final expression of a certain attitude or point of view
—White's admiration for the precarious manifestations of
nature in the city. For his love of New York included the
chance bird or tree that had managed to survive, as well
as the man-made ferment and pulse.

White begins by referring to some inane questions
about pigeons in *Promenade,* a hotel-sponsored publication. The author had asked if any one had ever seen a baby
pigeon in New York; if pigeons drink, and if so, where;
if they have nests; why they live in cities; and why they
like air-conditioners. The article ended as foolishly as it
began: " 'But pigeons, thank you for making my life so full
of wonder. Or is it Manhattan, *en toto* [*sic*], that does it?' "
(103).

Pretentiousness, bad spelling, ignorance about nature:
these were more than enough to get White started. He gives

generally sober and informative answers to the questions, but he adds a satirical jab now and then. To the question, "Are pigeons hatched fully grown?" he answers, "When hatched, a squab is about the size of a pigeon's egg." To the question about pigeons' drinking water in midtown Manhattan, he replies that they drink water in all five boroughs and gives an accurate account of where they could find water. White's pleasant drawings illustrating where pigeons liked to live in the city reveal still more of his accurate observations of their life.

Toward the end of the essay White tackled the expression "en toto": it doesn't turn up in his reference books, he says, but he did know a gorilla once named M'Toto. But beneath his mild scorn for the ignorant and unobservant, beneath even his close observation of pigeons, lay his special admiration for the tenacity of non-human life in the city. Like the tree in "The Second Tree from the Corner," the pigeon is a reminder to man that he is not the sole occupant even of his cities. Pigeons, like trees, or like the song of a bird in a city park, hold the promise of life—a promise for men as well as plants and animals: "The egg miraculous upon the ledge, the bird compact upon the egg, its generous warmth, its enviable patience, its natural fortitude and grace" (109).

## IV  *Time*

The last two essays to be discussed, among the best in *The Points of My Compass*, concern the circularity of time. The first, "The Ring of Time" (March 22, 1956) is, for the main part, a description of a practice session of John Ringling North's circus at its winter headquarters in Sarasota, Florida. At first, in a desultory scene, a woman of forty or so guides a brown circus horse around the practice ring. With the entry of the woman's daughter the scene comes alive. Sixteen or seventeen, "cleverly proportioned, deeply browned by the sun, dusty, eager, and almost naked," the daughter got on the horse, did some routine tricks, but mostly just stood on its back as it cantered around the ring. To the microcosm of the circus she brought one of those moments of enchantment when the circus "comes to a point, as through a burning glass, in the activity and destiny of a single performer" (53).

The scene was plain, natural: "the enchantment grew not out of anything that happened or was performed but out of something that seemed to go round and around and around with the girl, attending her, a steady gleam in the shape of a circle—a ring of ambition, of happiness, of youth." But, White sadly observes, in a week all will be changed, almost all lost: "The girl would wear makeup, the horse would wear gold, the ring would be painted, the bark would be clean for the feet of the horse, the girl's feet would be clean for the slippers she'd wear" (54).

The scene, with its circularity, makes White conscious of time: "She will never be as beautiful as this again," he thinks; she was too young to know that time does not move in a circle; she was "at that enviable moment in life . . . when she believes she can go once around the ring . . . and at the end be exactly the same age as at the start." And, as in "Once More to the Lake," or as in "Zoo Revisited," White moves back and forth in time; he sees the girl twenty-five years hence as the mother in the center, and then as she is at the moment, secure in the belief that the "ring of time was perfectly formed, changeless, predictable . . . ."

The rest of the essay, when White turns to other matters, is not notable; but the few pages about the girl and the central image of the ring show his thoughts about time vividly and with feeling. There is a ring of time in the plan of the whole book, with its reports from the points of White's compass. And it is not surprising that the last essay in the book, "The Years of Wonder" (March 13, 1961), takes the reader back to White's first years after college and particularly to his trip to Alaska—something White had only touched upon before. White tells us, in the opening of "The Years of Wonder," that, when Alaska achieved statehood, he looked into the journal he had kept while journeying to Alaska, "hoping to discover in its faded pages something instructive about the new state" (205). As he says, a reader might not find much about Alaska in the account he wrote, but he might find something about White and about the 1920's.

"The Years of Wonder" is, then, as White says, a "delayed account—some thirty-seven years late" (205). We can assume a certain degree of accident in the writing of "The Years of Wonder"—White has more often than not used contemporary events as a starting point for his essays, and he may really have wanted to write something appropriate to the new state of Alaska. But, this being among White's last essays, and one of his best, we may also assume that he was finally ready to deal with that most important part of his life. He says that during the Alaska trip he "felt more alive than I had ever felt before."

In other essays White had returned to earlier times—his early dating, his unrest over what part to play in World War I, his recollections of childhood, his adolescent queries about sex. We see in these accounts White's sense of the transiency of life; we see also, from his half-belief in the cyclical quality of life, the ring of time, that he has faith, or something close to it, in permanency. All of his reports of the past may not be in yet, all the points of his compass not yet revealed, but I suspect that his major themes have been stated; *The Points of My Compass*, in its subject and structure, is a fitting and impressive summation. In space, it is a microcosm of his world; in time, a symbol of the unity and coherence of human experience, where youth and age, city and country, past and present, come together. The book is ultimately White's plea for a vital life where the means do not become ends, where gadgets do not create more problems than they solve, where the "advances" of science do not destroy all possibility of real advance because they have destroyed life itself.

CHAPTER *9*

# *The Elements of Style*

A LTHOUGH White has written little since *The Points of My Compass*, a few items merit discussion before we turn to his prose style. One item, a speech on freedom that White recorded for the Voice of America series at station WLBZ, Bangor, Maine, on July 1, 1961, opens with references to the problems forced on mankind by science. We may, White says, be planning to send a man to the moon, but "in this fantastic age of discovery and of turmoil, freedom is still our basic need, our guiding urge, and our best hope. . . . Our task, then, is not to adjust the blessings of liberty to a time of fantastic adventure; our task is to hold these modern fantasies to their proper role, so they will serve, not destroy, the free spirit and the emerging individual."[1]

One fundamental right of man is privacy, he says—a right Americans have enjoyed; a right about which other peoples of the world have only dreamed. This right, White fears, is being threatened—by the supersonic jet whose shock waves invade his house "without a search warrant" or by nuclear testing by the United States and Russia when "a dangerous debris settled over all mankind, descending in the rain, violating the fields and streams, a threat to everyone's privacy and to everyone's health."[2] "In this twentieth century," White concludes, "we must make sure that Man's good sense keeps pace with his ingenuity. Privacy is still more precious than the moon. We must make sure that the speed of sound does not shatter the world's dishes, and that the age of speed does not destroy the age of reason."[3]

Simple, clear, and expressed in familiar terms, White's speech is effective. If our privacy is being invaded far more in 1973 than it was in 1961, it is no reflection on White, just sad evidence that his voice, like the voices of others, has been competing with powerful and sinister forces that reason seems powerless to combat.

Another social comment had to do with DDT. In a short poem, borrowing its style from Oliver Goldsmith's "The Deserted Village," White comments wryly on the discovery by an ornithologist in 1965 that in fifty-three eagles' nests, only four eaglets were found; in undeveloped eagles' eggs were traces of "DDT, DDE, and other poisons."[4] A few years later, White turned to birds again, in a pleasant retrospective excursion through Edward Howe Forbush's *Birds of Massachusetts and Other New England States.*[5] In another retrospective essay, printed in *Ford Times,* he wrote of his love of sailing and of his reluctant feeling that his sailing days were probably over.[6]

Half a dozen other items have appeared, and now and then a contribution to "Notes and Comment." Two pleasant essays, mostly about the geese on White's farm, recapture the spirit of *One Man's Meat.* In another essay, one of two that White wrote for *The New York Times* "Topics" department, White attempts to face the end-of-the-year questions: "What happened? What went sour? What did I do wrong?" The essay, published December 30, 1967, deals with some obvious problems: drugs, air and water pollution, disruption in our cities, the Viet Nam War. White, perhaps to the disappointment of some of his readers, has nothing very dramatic by way of answers, nothing especially invigorating or inspiring. The Viet Nam War he finds not immoral but amoral: "All war is amoral, and will continue to be amoral until some decent substitute is established to settle the things that must be settled and defend what has to be maintained." White repeats some of his doubts about progress—"Much that was hailed as progress has picked up the odor of retrogression"—and concludes on a hopeful note: "I believe our races can and will live peaceably and sensibly together. If I were to doubt these things I couldn't last the night out." The familiar dream will come true, he says; the "sky will again be bright, as it was many years ago on a memorable evening when the curtain rose on the first act of 'Oklahoma!' and the sounds of the earth were like music."

The questions are almost too big for answers, and perhaps hope is all we can have. Still, White seems remote here. *Oklahoma!* is not quite the right symbol, the "familiar dream" not the right one. For many people today, the "familiar dream" has too many ironic overtones to be viable. White was right enough in spirit, but for once the rhetoric was wrong. Perhaps his nostalgia for the "mythic past," as Wright Morris calls it,[7] obscured for him some of the sharper realities of the disintegrating present. At any rate, the vigor of *The Wild Flag* essays, as well as the depth and eloquence of the best of *One Man's Meat* or *The Points of My Compass*, is missing.

## I  *Style: William Strunk, Jr., and E. B. White*

On July 15, 1957, White wrote a sketch for *The New Yorker* entitled "Will Strunk." Beginning as a rambling account of the mosquito problems in White's New York apartment, it turns into a nostalgic tribute to Professor William Strunk, Jr., late of Cornell University, and to Strunk's book on rhetoric, *The Elements of Style*. The essay, reprinted in *The Points of My Compass*, had unexpected repercussions. Strunk's work, a short, precise guide to writing, free of jargon and written with a respect for the reader's intelligence and needs, had been used at Cornell in White's day but had later passed out of circulation, the fate of most such books. The Macmillan Company, however, expressed an interest in reprinting the work, and asked White to revise and amplify it. The task took White a year; when the book was published in 1959, it achieved an immediate and continuing popularity; it is still used in some high schools, and in many colleges and universities. In accounting for the book's popularity, White notes that it was a "right and wrong" book that "arrived on the scene at a time when a wave of reaction was setting in against the permissive school of rhetoric

. . . . The little book climbed on this handy wave and rode it in" *(The Points of My Compass,* 122).

White's *New Yorker* sketch became, with a few changes, the introduction of the book; he made some revisions to the book itself, and added a final chapter, "An Approach to Style." White, giving much good advice to the student, avoids the pitfall of considering style as something separable or isolated: "The beginner," he says, "should approach style warily, realizing that it is himself he is approaching" *(The Elements of Style,* 55). Many of his examples in this chapter are felicitous, and he generally manages to be precise and helpful, without being dogmatic. "Do not dress words up by adding *ly* to them, as though putting a hat on a horse," he writes, giving examples of "overly," "firstly," and "muchly." Nor could anyone help admiring a piece of advice toward the end of the chapter: "No one can write decently who is distrustful of the reader's intelligence, or whose attitude is patronizing" (70). And once and for all, we can hope, White and Strunk cut through years of confusion about the *'s* in singular possessives. Their simple rule is: "Form the possessive singular of nouns by adding *'s.*" (We see, for example, *"Dickens's"* a lot more than we used to, and we can give a silent word of thanks to "the little book.")

Curiously, this chapter about style is not one of White's effective pieces. It is not always clear, it is sometimes inconsistent, and it is repetitious in a way rare for White. Perhaps to get away from the dogmatism or jargon of some books on rhetoric, perhaps to give a feeling of ease and informality, he fell victim, for example, to the phrase "of course," which turns up a number of times in the chapter. He uses the word "cadence" to explain the effectiveness of Lincoln's "four-score and seven," although earlier in the chapter he had rejected the term: "We could, of course, talk about 'rhythm' and 'cadence,' but the talk would be vague and unconvincing" (53). And White, generally a model of precision, is far from achieving it when he advises that "although there is no substitute for merit in writing, clarity comes closest to being one" (65). "Merit" is left vague and undefined.

These may be niggling observations, but the point is that they are precisely the sort of observations we can rarely make about White's writing. We notice the slips because they are so rare elsewhere. White was probably aware of some of these matters, for in the postscript to the sketch on Strunk in *The Points of My Compass,* he said that his work on *The Elements of Style* took him a lot longer than he had expected: "I discovered that for all my fine talk I was no match for the parts of speech—was, in fact, over my depth and in trouble. Not only that, I felt uneasy posing as an expert on rhetoric, when the truth is I write by ear, always with difficulty and seldom with any exact notion of what is taking place under the hood" (122). White concludes his chapter on style perceptively, but he seems to be writing for himself or another artist, rather than for a freshman struggling with his weekly theme. "The whole duty of a writer," he says, "is to please and satisfy himself, and the true writer always plays to an audience of one. Let him start sniffing the air, or glancing at the Trend Machine, and he is as good as dead, although he may make a nice living." However, there are many good technicians with few or none of White's gifts who have written, and will continue to write, adequate and unexciting books for college English courses. The "little book," a necessary and memorable corrective, continues popular; a second edition appeared in 1972.

White's edition of *The Elements of Style* leads us to a basic question in any study of E. B. White—what are the elements of *his* style? An analysis of a writer's style is not an easy matter, but in the case of White we can begin, at least, with what I think is a clear point: White did not write as he did because of *The New Yorker.* Certain critics, and others, through some group of associations or prejudices that we will not explore, have glibly assumed that there is a *New Yorker* short story, a *New Yorker* poem, and so on. If White writes for *The New Yorker,* his style, according to this argument, is *The New Yorker* style. There may be a respectable argument for the proposition that there is a *New Yorker* short story;[8] but, if there is a style in the "Notes and Comment" department of the magazine, it is a style E. B. White created, not a style he felt constrained to follow.

Nonetheless, a few critics have tried to account for White's style in terms of *The New Yorker*. Herbert Gold, in a review of *The Points of My Compass*, speaks of White's "burden of grafting a Thoreauvian blend of stoical abstention and poetic concern onto *The New Yorker's* peculiarly discreet diction." He speaks also of *The New Yorker's* dislike of "strong emotion strongly expressed"; finally, he says, "White has been one of the architects of *The New Yorker* style, and also one of its victims."[9] Joseph Wood Krutch, in a review of *The Second Tree from the Corner*, takes a more moderate view. White, he says "writes with the almost finicky awareness of 'good usage' which it is said Mr. Ross . . . insisted upon. But once all this has proved that he 'belongs' he can be permitted to indulge what would otherwise seem the wildest eccentricity." But Krutch concludes that, it would hardly do to explain White "in terms of *The New Yorker* when you have to explain a good deal of *The New Yorker* in terms of him."[10]

This last comment, close to the truth of the matter, expresses a view a whole group of critics have taken. Stanley E. Hyman, for example, says of the "Notes and Comment" department: "The chief author of this page for many years, and the man who seems to have established its highly stylized form as an extension of his own personality, was E. B. White." And he says of the *One Man's Meat* essays (which White had written for *Harper's*) that it would "be hard to find a better exhibit of the magazine's [*The New Yorker's*] editorial characteristics than these essays."[11] In other words, White wrote as he wanted to write, whatever the publication.

To W. J. Weatherby, White gave *The New Yorker* "its voice";[12] Russell Maloney considers White as the inventor of the Comments style; Nat Hentoff, writing recently on another matter, notes that "the myth of *The New Yorker* 'style' is a myth. I have never been told how to write for the magazine, and accordingly, one of the reasons I enjoy writing for *The New Yorker* is that I feel entirely free to be myself, for good or ill. My experience is not atypical, according to other *New Yorker* writers I know."[14]

Finally, and most important, is the testimony of White himself, who told Roderick Nordell, " 'I think the only decent way to write is to write without patronizing anybody. . . . I've been lucky, I've never been asked to write in any particular way. . . . *The New Yorker* is a wonderful example of how a thing can succeed if you don't try to adjust.' "[15] White's style, we can safely conclude, developed freely as an expression of himself and of all those forces, impossible ever to understand fully, that make a man a writer. "Who knows," wrote Scott Elledge, "where he got his taste, or how to account for it? No doubt he learned from such 'teachers' as Professor Strunk at Cornell, editor Harold Ross at *The New Yorker,* and editor Katharine White in Maine and Manhattan. In various essays he has admired Ring Lardner, FPA, and James Thurber. Not only in 'Walden' but throughout *One Man's Meat* it is easy to hear what sound like echoes of Thoreau. But there is no telling where he found the passion to write well in a style free from the rhetoric associated with the phrase 'literary merit.' "[16]

If it is not easy to account for White's style, it is also not easy to describe it, though that must be my concern now. Certainly one key to its perfection is his choice of words. J. W. Fuller, in his closely written and full study of E. B. White's style, notes that, when White has waiters, taxi drivers, news-reel announcers, junk-shop proprietors, or nurses talking, they use words in keeping with their role.[17] We can rarely say of a White dialogue that a bartender, let us say, would not have talked as he does. White has a good ear for music, and he has a good ear too for words, for accent, and for American sloppiness — as, for example, the radio announcer he heard predicting "innermitten" storms, or the one who said the streets of Providence had been "unindated."

Unlike some writers, White has few words or expressions that he keeps using. It is remarkable, for example, that for over a twenty-year period, while he was writing substantial parts of "Notes and Comment," there were only two or three instances when he opened a comment with the same word or phrase. And even those expressions or words of which he appears to be fond are used so rarely as to be scarcely noticed.

What is striking about White's use of words is not so much the individual choice but the context in which the choice appears—his brilliant use of contrast, his use of the specific word to make a generalization or an abstraction clear, his figures of speech drawn from clear observation of nature or daily life. When he speaks for example of the people whose names appear in Forbush's *Birds of Massachusetts and Other New England States,* he says they "have achieved immortality; their names are imbedded in the text . . . as firmly as a bottle cap in a city pavement" (46). He likes the honesty of Maine speech, compared to what he hears at parties in town, where "there wasn't a remark in the room that couldn't be brought down with a common pin" *(One Man's Meat,* 193). And he occasionally likes to use human comparisons in describing animals, as when he describes chilly baby chickens "standing round with their collars turned up, blowing on their hands and looking like a snow-removal gang under the El on a bitter winter's midnight" (235).

In a more subtle sense, beyond that of rhetorical effectiveness, contrast is at the heart of White's style; and, because style is, after all, the man, it is partly at least at the heart of E. B. White. White often describes country things in city terms, and city things in country terms; and, although we cannot assume (as Caroline Spurgeon wanted to assume in her study of Shakespeare's metaphors) that a writer's beliefs can be inferred through his figures of speech, still *something* is revealed. And just as there is a dualism in White about the city and the country—his love for Maine and his love for New York City—so there is a tonal dualism in White. If he found it hard to write anything long or sustained, he seems also to have found it hard to maintain a consistent tone of seriousness or of lightheartedness.

He can talk seriously, for example, about the Southern attitude toward blacks and then say, "I have to laugh when I think about the sheer inconsistency of the Southern attitude about color: the Negro barred from the movie house because of color, the orange with 'color added' for its ultimate triumph." He concludes by commenting that he could design a float for some Southern fête: "It would contain a beautiful Negro woman riding with other bathing beauties and stamped with the magical words, Color Added" (*One Man's Meat*, 220-21). Or, as in the end of "Once More to the Lake," he could bring a sudden reality, almost the taste of death, to what has seemed in the main a happy reminiscence about childhood.

White himself comments on one aspect of his dualism: "Half the time we feel blissfully wedded to the modern scene, in love with its every mood, amused by its every joke, imperturbable in the face of its threat, bent on enjoying it to the hilt. The other half of the time we are the fusspot moralist, suspicious of all progress, resentful of change, determined to right wrongs, correct injustices, and save the world even if we have to blow it to pieces in the process" (*The Second Tree from the Corner*, 121). Or, as J. W. Fuller has put it, he has a spirit of playfulness and fun that balances his "negativism and pessimism . . . . His impulsive outbursts are balanced by close reasoning."[18]

We can say fairly that White's habit of shifting tone gives great charm to much of his writing; it is also fair to note that occasionally the shifts are not entirely happy. The passage about race and color, for example, might seem today too light, almost careless. White is vulnerable here, and this is the sort of shift for which he has on occasion been criticized. Webster Schott, for example, objects to the ending of "Sootfall and Fallout" where White concludes a discussion of nuclear testing and fallout problems with "The character of rain has changed, the joy of watching it soak the waiting earth has been diminished, and the whole meaning and worth of gardens has been brought into question." Schott parodied what he felt was the trivial ending with "Developments down there [Cuba] have brought the whole meaning and worth of cigar smoking into question."[19]

Herbert Gold, who was also bothered by the same sort of thing, found *Points of My Compass* "brilliant sentence by sentence, convincing paragraph by paragraph, but [it] occasionally fades out into whimsy over the long stretch of an essay."[20] But comments like these about White are rare; and, although we can admit the specific justice of them, we should not be surprised. The truth is that over the long stretch of White's work, the combination of serious-ness and whimsy, or of the minute and the momentous,[21] is effective, and at times profoundly true. Because human experience itself is a curious mixture of shifting tones and moods there is a basic honesty and wisdom in White's writing; he reveals himself as a man unafraid of surface contradictions or of simple and natural responses.

This honesty in White leads to other qualities of his style: clarity and spontaneity. Of course he was a master of the technical aspects of English, and J. W. Fuller in one part of his study of White's style has made an admi-rable demonstration of his skill in the use of commas, semi-colons, sentence types, paragraphs, and so forth. But these are the tools, the means, and not the end. The grammarian or rhetorician recognizes White's skill; the general reader understands what White is saying.

White takes an expert's pleasure in finding himself or others falling prey to the traps that lie in wait for the writer of English. The following passage shows his sharp ear for clarity:

The English language is always sticking a foot out to trip a man. Every week we get thrown, writing merrily along. Even Dr. Canby, a careful and experienced craftsman, got thrown in his own editorial [in the Saturday Review]. He spoke of 'the makers of textbooks who are nearly always reactionary, and often un-scholarly in denying the right to change to a language that has always been changing . . . ' In this case the word 'change,' quietly sandwiched in between a couple of 'to's,' unexpectedly exploded the whole sentence. Even inverting the phrases wouldn't have helped. If he had started out 'In denying to a language . . . the right to change,' it would have come out this way: 'In denying to a language that has always been changing the right to change . . . ' English usage is sometimes more than mere taste, judgment, and education—sometimes it's sheer luck, like getting across a street.

(The Second Tree from the Corner, 151)

Luck or intuition, good writers have it. White, never much in favor of attempts to regularize or systematize English, and suspicious of those who count words and speak of "levels of readability," has probably been pleased that, after some initial enthusiasms, considerable disillusion has set in among those working on translating machines and the like.

If we take as the final judgment the opinions of other writers and of editors, the standing of White is clear. J. W. Fuller, for example, noted that, in a survey of forty college anthologies chosen at random, there were, excluding poems, short stories, and plays, more selections by E. B. White than by any other author. Today, thirteen years after Fuller's survey, an informal search shows that White is still one of the commonly selected writers, although his writings tend now to turn up in selections of essays, rather than in general college anthologies. Also, his more sensitive pieces, and what seem to me his best—"Once More to the Lake," "The Door," and "The Ring of Time"— are included more frequently than when Fuller wrote. In addition, many of White's works have been reprinted in trade editions.

CHAPTER *10*

# The Significance of E. B. White

I N a famous essay about Emerson, written to be delivered as a lecture during his American tour of 1883-84, Matthew Arnold began negatively. Emerson was not, he said, a great poet, a great writer, a great philosopher; but he was "the friend and aider of those who would live in the spirit."[1] I would not say precisely the same thing about White, yet Arnold's approach is not inappropriate; for it must be admitted at the outset that White has not written great poems, great novels, great plays, or great short stories. As these are the genres most talked about and admired by today's critics, we might wonder what there was left for White to be.

First, White has written a few short stories that come close to being great: "The Door," "The Second Tree from the Corner." He is without question one of the best essayists writing; there is little better in that form than "Once More to the Lake," "The Ring of Time," or "The Years of Wonder." *Charlotte's Web,* still a best seller, is a classic among children's stories and may well turn out to be the longest remembered of his works. In addition, White has written with passion of his hope for world unity—a passion that seems now nostalgic; a hope that seems both bright and receding. And some of his work has an eerie, prophetic quality. His fanciful projections about pollution, the breakdown of our cities, the tastelessness of television advertising—all these are taking on a frightening reality. But at present there are further reasons for valuing White highly.

For one thing, the significance of White is closely tied to that of *The New Yorker*. White modestly underestimates his role on the magazine, but the evidence on the other side, presented at the beginning of Chapter III, is too compelling to be rejected. Whatever the importance of Harold Ross, James Thurber, and Katharine White, E. B. White established the form and set the tone for the "Notes and Comment" department—the heart of *The New Yorker*. Only when we have read through "Notes and Comment" from 1927 to the late 1940's do we see the magnitude of White's achievement. He contributed more than any other writer, and he frequently wrote most, if not all, of the department. A good guess is that many of the readers of *The New Yorker* turn first to "Notes and Comment." White was vital in attracting readers, and only when a solid readership is established can a magazine develop and attract increasing numbers of good writers and critics.

Of course White contributed more than the items in "Notes and Comment." He started his *New Yorker* job, actually, by writing tag lines for the newsbreaks department; he is still doing it. Furthermore, the majority of his stories and sketches appeared first in *The New Yorker*. These contributions, especially in the early days of the magazine, were important, as Allen Churchill has noted: "The magazine did not really thrive until it developed its own young writers in the early 1930's. The best of these—or at least the ones who gave *The New Yorker* its celebrated off-center approach—were Thurber and E. B. White. And, to a great extent, Wolcott Gibbs."[2]

We can surely say that White was one of the main reasons for the success of *The New Yorker*. The larger issue, however, the importance of the magazine itself, is not so easily settled. The magazine has attracted intensely loyal supporters, and it has also had its severe critics. Although this study is not the place for a prolonged analysis of *The New Yorker*, some comments are necessary because White's significance is closely connected with that of *The New Yorker*. One problem about the magazine is that to some people it is mainly a source of urbane, sophisticated humor. Oscar Cargill, writing in 1941, illustrates something of this

attitude when he says that *"The New Yorker,* which has been
the chief organ of expression for the younger wits since
its founding in 1925, is a better humorous magazine than
such predecessors as *Puck, Life,* and *Judge."*[3] *The New
Yorker,* however, had really very little connection with
*Puck, Judge,* or the first *Life.* Leo Gurko, even more limited
in his evaluation, grants that it was "the wittiest and most
urbanely intelligent periodical in the United States,"
but he concludes that it was "in the end a brilliant monument to negativism and creates effects no more durable
than the absurdities of the hour."[4]

We can easily find comments of a different sort. Henry
Steele Commager, in *The American Mind,* says that in *The
New Yorker* "Americans could boast a magazine as liberal,
lively, and intelligent as anything published in the western world, and as surely one of the glories of American civilization as *The New York Times* or *The Atlantic Monthly."*[5] And James Thurber, conceding that a number of big
names were absent from *The New Yorker* — William Faulkner,
John Dos Passos, Ernest Hemingway — adds that many fine
writers *were* published in it: Edward Newhouse, Irwin Shaw,
J. D. Salinger, Jean Stafford, John Cheever, and Mary
McCarthy.[6]

This is an impressive enough list, and others could be
added, notably John Updike and Vladimir Nabokov. Ultimately, however, the significance of *The New Yorker*
rests as much on its non-fiction as on its fiction. From
1925 to 1950, for example, two hundred and fifty-five
books, many of them non-fiction, first appeared as extended
articles in *The New Yorker.*[7] This total, much expanded
by 1973, includes such memorable works as John Hersey's
*Hiroshima,* Edmund Wilson's *The Dead Sea Scrolls
1947-1969,* Rachel Carson's *The Sea around Us* and *The
Silent Spring,* and Truman Capote's *In Cold Blood.* Almost
equally important are the contributions of A. J. Liebling,
E. J. Kahn, Berton Roueché, Richard Rovere, and Robert
Shaplen.

What certainly strikes any student of *The New Yorker*
is the reliability and thoroughness of its non-fiction. The
magazine's insistence on accuracy is well enough known;

in fact, *The New Yorker* invented a new literary form of
major importance: the fully and carefully drawn "Profiles."
The scope of these articles is striking, from whaling to the
steamship *Great Eastern,* from studies of the caste system in India to a series of articles about the moon—for
all of these topics, to mention a small sample, *The New
Yorker* has become an important source. White has not had a
great deal to do with this aspect of *The New Yorker;* no one
would claim that he was responsible for *all* of the magazine.
What I have tried to establish is that White was a central
figure in the growth of one of the country's major period-
icals.

Few admirers of E. B. White, however, would be content to
let his significance rest on his connection with *The New
Yorker;* or on his worth as a stylist; or as a writer of sketches,
short stories, or children's books. He is equally important
as the spokesman of our times for the right of privacy, a
right threatened by the population explosion, by devices
for snooping, and by repressive measures instituted through
the fear of violence in our society. It is a right that many
people of the world have never known, and never will
know, and it is a right in danger of being forgotten by
some of those who once understood it. It is a right, finally,
that may turn out to be the most essential ingredient of
freedom as we have known it. More fashionable today than
privacy are commitment, involvement, community dialogue,
confrontation. We must be a member of something, have a
label—and in some measure cease to be an individual.
Perhaps privacy is an outmoded or irrelevant concept in
today's world. If so, White's championing of it is simply
another aspect of his nostalgia for the past, and it may be
that we will have to give up privacy; but in so doing we
must reconcile ourselves to becoming another sort of being
than we have striven thus far to become.

White is, in E. M. Forster's sense of the word, an aris-
tocrat—one of the aristocracy of "the sensitive, the con-
siderate and the plucky"—and he speaks for those like
himself. He speaks indeed for more than the right of privacy, for ultimately it is an attitude, a way of life, that
White represents. There are no handy words to describe

that attitude, and it doesn't appeal to extremists, enthu-
siasts, labelers, and joiners. To some today White might
seem to lack commitment; he was not a bohemian or an
expatriate in the 1920's, or a Marxist in the 1930's. He
didn't belong to the Algonquin group in New York; he
was not Freudian, a semanticist, a technocrat. He fervently
believed in world government, but he was not formally
aligned with any world government organizations. He
avoided literary cults and clichés; he does mention
briefly some of the writers who influenced his prose style
in his immediate post-college days, but it is difficult
to find the mature White writing or thinking in any way
but his own. In fact, he seldom refers to other writers.[8]

White speaks for those who have taken, like himself, the
often lonely role of the true individualist. He gives strength
to those who find the role difficult, who find it hard to
resist putting on a badge or acquiring a label, but who do
resist. Surely such a spokesman has a significant part
to play in a society in which pressures to conform are great
and in which even non-conformity turns upon itself and
produces often the ultimate conformist. Although White
may sometimes hold a middle position, his role is not
that of the defender of compromise. But, unlike the professional liberal, or the professional conservative, he
doesn't scorn the middle position; and, when he sees
cause, he is not afraid to abandon whatever position he has
taken. He embodies tolerance without condescension, understanding without oversimplification, individualism without eccentricity.

*Notes and References*

# Notes and References

*Chapter One*

1. Letter to the author from E. B. White, November 4, 1964.
2. Letter from Barrett Brady to E. B. White, October 25, 1945, in the Cornell collection.
3. "A True Dog Story," *St. Nicholas,* XLI (1914), 1045.
4. "The Writer as a Private Man," *Christian Science Monitor,* October 31, 1962, p. 9.
5. Susan Frank, interview with E. B. White in *The Cornell Daily Sun,* October 9, 1964, p. S-2.
6. *Ibid.*
7. Morris Bishop, *A History of Cornell* (Ithaca, 1962), p. 432.
8. The entry for White in the 1921 Cornellian is as follows:
   Elwyn Brooks White, "Andy," Mount Vernon. Arts and Sciences. Age, twenty-one. Prepared at Mt. Vernon High School. Four years at Cornell. ΦΓΔ; Aleph Samach; Quill and Dagger; ΣΔΧ; Sophomore Cotillion Committee; Junior Smoker Committee; Navy Day Hop Committee 3, 4; Freshman Advisory Committee; Spring Day Committee; Senior Ball Committee; *The Cornell Daily Sun* Board 1, 2, 3, Editor-in-Chief 4; Manuscript Club.
9. Letter to the author from Dale Mitchell, July 14, 1963.
10. This special task was imposed upon members for the infraction of a club rule.
11. "The Manuscript Club," *The Cornell Era,* LIII (June 11, 1921), 9.
12. For the account of this incident I am indebted to E. B. White, who has related the whole matter in a letter to me of July 10, 1968.
13. *The Critic,* December 7, 1920.
14. *One Man's Meat,* ed. Morris Bishop (New York, 1950), p. vi.

15. *Ibid.*

16. *Ibid.*, p. v.

17. Frank, p. S-2.

18. Letter from E. B. White to Martin W. Sampson III, April 24, 1961. Privately held.

19. Frank, p. S-2.

20. Letter to the author from Howard Cushman, September 7, 1963.

21. *Louisville Herald,* May 14, 1922. I am indebted to Virginia C. Walker of the University of Kentucky Library for finding this.

22. "Speaking of Counterweights," *The Points of My Compass* (New York, 1962), p. 10.

23. Dale Kramer, *Ross and The New Yorker* (Garden City, 1951), p. 195; Ralph Ingersoll, *"The New Yorker," Fortune,* X (August, 1934), 72-86, 90, 92, 97; James Thurber, "E. B. W." *Saturday Review of Literature,* XVIII (October 15, 1938), 8-9.

24. Typed note by E. B. White in the Cornell collection.

25. Clippings from *The Seattle Times* in the Cornell collection.

26. Robert K. Murray, *Red Scare* (Minneapolis, 1955), pp. 206-07.

27. Letter to the author from E. B. White, July 17, 1963.

28. "Where do New Eras Go?" *Magazine of Business,* LIV (November, 1928), 505.

29. "A Stratagem for Retirement," *Holiday* (March, 1956), p. 85.

30. J. Thorne Smith, "Advertising," in *Civilization in the United States,* ed. Harold E. Stearns (New York, 1922), p. 385.

31. "Noontime of an Advertising Man," *The New Yorker,* XXV (June 25, 1949), p. 26.

32. "Urgency of an Agency," *The New Republic,* LXVI (April 1, 1931), 180.

33. "Noontime," p. 26.

34. James Thurber, *The Years with Ross* (Boston, 1959), p. 92.

35. Frank, p. S-8.

36. *Ibid.*, p. S-2.

37. *Here Is New York* (New York, 1949), p. 31.

38. Ingersoll, p. 86.

## *Chapter Two*

1. *One Man's Meat,* Introduction by Morris Bishop (New York, 1950), p. vii.

2. *Ibid.*, p. 118.

3. Letter to the author, May 24, 1973.

4. David McCord, *Yale Review*, XXVIII (December, 1938), 393.

5. *Ibid.*

6. Leonard Bacon, "Humors and Careers," *Saturday Review of Literature*, XX (April 29, 1939), 4.


*Chapter Three*

1. Russell Maloney, "Tilley the Toiler," *Saturday Review*, XXX (August 30, 1947), 9.

2. Stanley E. Hyman, "The Urban New Yorker," *The New Republic*, CVII (July 20, 1942), 90.

3. Ralph Ingersoll, *"The New Yorker,"* *Fortune*, X (August, 1934), 85.

4. *One Man's Meat*, ed. Morris Bishop, p. vii.

5. Introduction, *Is Sex Necessary?* (New York, 1950), p. xii.

6. Frederick J. Hoffman, *The Twenties* (New York, 1962), p. 229.

7. *Ibid.*, p. 232.

8. These comments were reprinted in *Every Day Is Saturday* (New York, 1934), pp. 32, 37, 98.

9. Maxwell Geismar, *Writers in Crisis* (Boston, 1942), p. viii.

10. James Thurber, "E. B. W.," *Saturday Review of Literature* (October 5, 1938), 9.

11. In a comment on the margin of my manuscript White has written: "The parable was based on the news of an attempt to rescue some residents of Tangier Island in Chesapeake Bay one cold winter. I merely overstated what actually happened."


*Chapter Four*

1. Unless otherwise indicated, references in the text to *One Man's Meat* are to Morris Bishop's edition (New York, 1950).

2. Enck, *et al.*, *The Comic in Theory and Practice* (New York, 1960).


*Chapter Five*

1. Letter to the author, August 4, 1968.

2. "A Federalist at Three A. M.," *The Blue Flag* (published by the students of the Dalton School), XIV (April, 1950), 4.

3. About a third of the material in the Preface had appeared earlier in an article "The State of States," *Transatlantic,* January, 1945, pp. 28-31.

4. Roderick Nordell, "The Writer as a Private Man," *Christian Science Monitor,* October 31, 1962, p. 9.

5. There were a number of such studies before the date of *The Wild Flag;* for example, Edward Glover, *War, Sadism, and Pacifism* (1933); John Bowlby, *Personal Aggressiveness and War* (1939); Mark A. May, *A Social Psychology of War and Peace* (1943); and J. C. Flugel, *The Moral Paradox of Peace and War* (1941).

6. J. C. Flugel, *Man, Morals, and Society* (New York, 1961), p. 310.

7. For example, R. B. Perry, *One World in the Making* (1945); Emery Reves, *The Anatomy of Peace* (1945); J. T. Shotwell, *The Great Decision* (1944).

8. "Khrushchev and I," *The New Yorker,* XXXV (September 26, 1959), 41.

### Chapter Six

1. Letter to the author from Howard Cushman, October 27, 1963.

2. Malcolm Cowley, review of *Stuart Little, The New York Times Book Review,* October 28, 1945, p. 7.

3. "The Librarian Said It Was Bad for Children," *The New York Times,* March 6, 1966, sec. X, p. 19.

4. Cowley, p. 7.

5. Letter to the author, March 24, 1973.

6. Bennett Cerf, *Saturday Review,* XXXVI (January 3, 1953), 6.

### Chapter Seven

1. Russell Maloney, "Tilley the Toiler," *Saturday Review,* XXX (August 30, 1947), 10.

2. William Steinhoff, " 'The Door,': 'The Professor,' 'My Friend the Poet (Deceased),' 'The Washable House,' and 'The Man Out in Jersey,' " *College English,* XXIII (December, 1961), 229-32.

3. As Steinhoff suggested, White "could have read a graphic description of a new technique for this operation in *The New York Times* on March 9, 1939, where it is called 'a new kind of operation for correcting the "disease of civilization." ' " *College English,* p. 231.

4. *Ibid.*, p. 231.

5. Jane Harrison, *Mythology* (New York, 1963), p. 105.

6. Letter to the author, July 10, 1968.


*Chapter Nine*

1. "The Right of Privacy," ms. in Cornell collection, p. 1.

2. *Ibid.*, p. 3.

3. *Ibid.*, p. 4.

4. "The Deserted Nation," *The New Yorker*, XVII (October 8, 1966), 53.

5. "Annals of Birdwatching: Mr. Forbush's Friends," *The New Yorker*, XLII (February 26, 1966), 42-66.

6. "The Sea and the Wind that Blows," *Ford Times*, LVI (June, 1963), 2-6.

7. Wright Morris, *The Territory Ahead* (New York, 1957), p. 19.

8. See J. W. Aldridge, *After the Lost Generation* (New York, 1951), pp. 146-48; Allen Churchill, "Ross of *The New Yorker*," *The American Mercury*, LXVII (August, 1948), 177.

9. Herbert Gold, " 'The Points of My Compass: Letters from the East, the West, the North, the South,' by E. B. White," *Saturday Review*, XLV (November 24, 1962), 30.

10. Joseph W. Krutch, "The Profession of a New Yorker," *Saturday Review*, XXXVII (June 30, 1954), 16.

11. Stanley E. Hyman, "The Urban New Yorker," *The New Republic*, CVII (July 20, 1942), 90,91.

12. W. J. Weatherby, "A Modern Man of Walden," *The Manchester Guardian Weekly*, February 14, 1963, p. 14.

13. Russell Maloney, "Tilley the Toiler," *Saturday Reveiw*, XXX (August 30, 1947), 10.

14. Nat Hentoff, "Tom Wolfe and *The New Yorker*," *The Village Voice*, May 6, 1965, pp. 5, 10.

15. Roderick Nordell, "The Writer as a Private Man," *The Christian Science Monitor*, October 31, 1962, p. 9.

16. Scott Elledge, "*One Man's Meat* by E. B. White," *The Carleton Miscellany*, IV (Winter, 1964), 85.

17. J. W. Fuller, "Prose Style in the Essays of E. B. White," unpublished dissertation, University of Washington, 1959, p. 54.

18. *Ibid.*, p. 47.

19. Webster Schott, "E. B. White Forever," *The New Republic*, CXLVII (November 24, 1962), 24.

20. Gold, p. 30.

21. Cf. Fuller, p. 46.

## Chapter Ten

1. Matthew Arnold, *Prose and Poetry*, ed. Bouton (New York, 1927), p. 240.

2. Allen Churchill, "Harold Ross, Editor of *The New Yorker*," *Cosmopolitan*, CXXIV (May, 1948), 176.

3. Oscar Cargill, *Intellectual Americana* (New York, 1941), p. 514.

4. Leo Gurko, *Heroes, Highbrows and the Popular Mind* (Indianapolis, 1953), p. 137. In an earlier comment, Gurko had been more charitable: see *The Angry Decade* (New York, 1947), p. 175.

5. Henry Steele Commager, *The American Mind* (New Haven, 1950), p. 81.

6. James Thurber, *The Years with Ross* (Boston, 1959), pp. 75, 171.

7. Sydney S. Thomas, "*The New Yorker's* Contributions to the Book World During a Quarter Century," unpublished Master's thesis, University of Georgia, 1950. According to Thurber the figure was around four hundred by 1957, if one included collections of articles, stories, and drawings (*The Years with Ross*, p. 172).

8. "I was never a reader. I was arriving at conclusions almost independently of the entire history of the world." White, in an interview with Israel Shenker, *The New York Times*, July 11, 1969, p. 43.

*Selected Bibliography*

# Selected Bibliography

PRIMARY SOURCES

1.  Books and Collections

*Alice Through the Cellophane* (A pamphlet). New York: John Day, 1933.
*Another Ho-Hum.* New York: Farrar and Rinehart, 1932.
*Charlotte's Web.* New York: Harper & Bros., 1952.
*Every Day Is Saturday.* New York: Harper & Bros., 1934.
*Farewell to Model T.* New York: G. P. Putnam's Sons, 1936. (Based on a suggestion by Richard L. Strout. The author was given as Lee Strout White).
*The Fox of Peapack and Other Poems.* New York: Harper & Bros., 1938.
*Here Is New York.* New York: Harper & Bros., 1949.
*Ho-Hum: Newsbreaks from The New Yorker.* New York: Farrar and Rinehart, 1931.
*The Lady Is Cold.* New York: Harper & Bros., 1929.
*Is Sex Necessary?* New York: Harper & Bros., 1929.
*One Man's Meat.* New York: Harper & Bros., 1942.
————, A New and Enlarged Edition. New York: Harper & Brothers, 1944.
————, ed. Morris Bishop, Harper's Modern Classics. New York: Harper & Brothers, 1950.
*The Points of My Compass.* New York: Harper & Row, 1962.
*Quo Vadimus? or The Case for the Bicycle.* New York: Harper & Bros., 1939.
*The Second Tree from the Corner.* New York: Harper & Bros., 1954.
————, ed. W. W. Watt, Harper's Modern Classics, 1962.
*Stuart Little.* New York: Harper & Row, 1945.
*The Trumpet of the Swan.* New York: Harper & Row, 1970.
*The Wild Flag.* Boston: Houghton Mifflin Co., 1946.

2. Introductions and Miscellaneous

Jones, Roy E., *A Basic Chicken Guide for the Small Flock Owner*. New York: William Morrow & Co., 1944. Introduction by E. B. White.

Marquis, Don. *the lives and times of archy and mehitabel*. New York: Doubleday, 1950. Introduction by E. B. White.

Strunk, William, Jr. *The Elements of Style*. New York: Macmillan, 1959. Revisions, an Introduction, and a New Chapter on Writing by E. B. White.

————, *The Elements of Style*, Second Edition. New York: Macmillan, 1972.

Thurber, James. *The Owl in the Attic*. New York: Grosset & Dunlap, 1931. Introduction by E. B. White.

White, E. B. and White, Katharine S. (eds.). *A Subtreasury of American Humor*. New York: Coward-McCann, 1941.

White, E. B. *An E. B. White Reader*, ed. William W. Watt and Robert W. Bradford. New York: Harper & Row, 1966.


3. Uncollected Works (This list is far from complete.)

"Annals of Bird Watching: Mr. Forbush's Friends," *The New Yorker*, XLII (February 26, 1966), 42-66.

"A Blessed Event—I," *The New Yorker*, XI (January 25, 1936), 32-34.

"A Blessed Event—II," *The New Yorker*, XI (February 1, 1936), 31-35.

"The Class of 1921," *1921 Cornellian*, Cornell University, 1921, pp. 185-192.

"The Deserted Nation," *The New Yorker*, XLII (October 8, 1966, 53.

"Farmer White's Brown Eggs (Cont.)," *The New York Times* (December 31, 1971), p. 19.

"A Federalist at Three A.M.," *Blue Flag*, XIV (April, 1950), 4-6, (published by the students of the Dalton School).

"Fred on Space," *The New Yorker*, XXXIII (November 6, 1957), 46-47.

"How the Automobile Got into Bermuda," *The New Yorker*, XIV (April 2, 1938), 22-23.

"I Accept with Pleasure," *The New Yorker*, XIX (March, 1943), 16.

"I'd Send My Son to Cornell," *Our Cornell*, Ithaca: The Cayuga Press, 1939.

"Khrushchev and I," *The New Yorker*, XXXV (September 26, 1959), 39-41.

"Letter from the East," *The New Yorker*, XLVII (March 27, 1971), 35-37.

"Letter from the East," *The New Yorker*, XLVII (July 24, 1971), 27-29.

"The Librarian Said It Was Bad for Children," *The New York Times*, (March 6, 1966), p. 19.

"Love among the Foreign Offices," *The New Yorker*, XXII (February 1, 1947), 24.

[Maine Lobsterman]. Script for a documentary television film made by Omnibus CBS in 1954.

"The Manuscript Club," *The Cornell Era*, LIII (June 11, 1921), 9.

"Mood Men," *Reader's Digest* XXXIII (July, 1938), 87-89. (Condensed from *The New Yorker*, March 26, 1938.)

"Noontime of an Advertising Man," *The New Yorker*, XXV (June 25, 1949), 25-26.

"A Note," *The New Yorker*, XXVI (February 11, 1950), 31.

"A Reporter at Large: Beautiful upon a Hill," *The New Yorker*, XXI (May 12, 1945), 42, 44, 45.

"A Reporter at Large: The Eve of St. Francis," *The New Yorker* XXI (May 5, 1945), 44, 47.

Review of *Walden*. (An illustrated edition with photographs by Edwin Way Teele.) *The New Yorker*, XXII (December 28, 1946), 57-58.

"The Right of Privacy." A speech recorded at WLBZ, Bangor, Maine, July 1, 1961, for The Voice of America.

"The Sea and the Wind that Blows," *Ford Times*, LVI (June, 1963), 2-6.

"Seven Steps to Heaven," *The New Yorker*, XXXIII (September 7, 1957), 32-37.

"State of the States," *Transatlantic*, #17 (January, 1945), 28-31.

"A Stratagem for Retirement," *Holiday*, XIX (March, 1956), 84-87.

"Topics: An Act of Intellect to Turn the Year," *The New York Times*, (December 30, 1967), p. 22.

"Topics: Dear Mr. . . . ," *The New York Times*, (September 23, 1967), p. 30.

"Urgency of an Agency" *New Republic*, LXVI (April 1, 1931), 180-181.

"Was Lifted by Ears as Boy, No Harm Done," *The New Yorker*, XL (May 9, 1964), 38.

"Where are the Diabolos?" *Forum*, LXXXIII (January, 1930), 50-52.

"Where Do the New Eras Go?" *Magazine of Business,* LIV
(November, 1928), 505.
"You Can't Resettle Me," *Saturday Evening Post,* CCIX (October
10, 1936), 8-9, 91-92.


SECONDARY SOURCES

AARON, DANIEL. *Writers on the Left.* New York: Harcourt, Brace
& World, 1961. Standard work about influence of Communism
on American writers, particularly during the 1920's and 1930's.
ALDRIDGE, J. W. *After the Lost Generation.* New York: McGraw-
Hill, 1951. Good account of the literary background of 1930's
and 1940's. Speaks of the influence of *The New Yorker,* and
what he calls "the code" of *The New Yorker.*
———. *In Search of Heresy.* New York: McGraw-Hill, 1956. Post-
World War II background: quality of life, taste; shifting in-
terests of the novel from the 1920's and 1930's to the 1950's.
Broad, valuable study.
ALLEN, FREDERICK L. *Only Yesterday.* New York: Blue Ribbon
Books, 1931. Background of the 1920's; good material on advertising, on those who work in it, and on the disillusionment in the period.
BACON, LEONARD. "How to Break a Rib," *The Saturday Review
of Literature,* XXIV (November 22, 1941), 7-8. Brief comment on White; praises his unpretentious skill.
———. "Humors and Careers," *The Saturday Review of Literature,* XX (April 29, 1939), 3-4, 22. Discussion, in part,
of Thurber, White, and Nash; permanence in them found
lacking in many modern humorists.
BECK, WARREN. "E. B. White," *College English,* VII (April,
1946), 367-73. Appreciative comment on White; notes his
plucky independence. Valuable material on White's prose
style.
BISHOP, MORRIS. *A History of Cornell.* Ithaca: Cornell University Press, 1962. Best account of Cornell.
BLAIR, WALTER. *Horse Sense in American Humor.* Chicago: University of Chicago Press, 1942. American tradition of racy humor
and horse sense; comments on Benchley, Thurber, Perelman,
others.
CARGILL, OSCAR. *Intellectual America.* New York: Macmillan Co.,
1941. Useful background information on the 1920's and 1930's.

CARR, E. H. *The Twenty Years' Crisis, 1919-1939.* New York: Harper & Row, 1964. Good account of international politics.

CHOMSKY, NOAM. "Language and the Mind I," *The Columbia University Forum,* XI (Spring, 1968), 5-10. Fine article on the complexities of English.

CHURCHILL, ALLEN. "Harold Ross, Editor of *The New Yorker,*" *Cosmopolitan,* CXXIV (May, 1948), 46-47, 174-78. Asserts *The New Yorker* style result of Ross's insistence on accuracy and style; has some comments about the importance of Katharine White on *The New Yorker.*

COLBY, FRANK M. "Humour." *Civilization in the United States.* Ed. Harold Stearns. New York: Harcourt, Brace & Co., 1922. Expresses skepticism about the existence of humor in America.

COMMAGER, HENRY STEELE. *The American Mind.* New Haven: Yale University Press, 1950. Standard intellectual history.

COWLEY, MALCOLM. *Exile's Return.* New York: Viking Press, 1951. Standard account of "the lost generation."

DE VOTO, BERNARD. *The Literary Fallacy.* Boston: Little, Brown & Co., 1944. Notes that literature of 1920's did not give a true picture of American life (the "literary fallacy" is the assumption that literature embodies the content of a culture).

ELLEDGE, SCOTT. Review of *One Man's Meat. The Carleton Miscellany,* IV (Winter, 1964), 83-87. Thoughtful review; some perceptive remarks on White's style.

ENCK, JOHN, FORTER, ELIZABETH, and WHITLEY, ALVIN (eds.). *The Comic in Theory and Practice.* New York: Appleton-Century-Crofts, 1960. Valuable sourcebook; contains many classic statements on humor.

FLUGEL, J.C. *Man, Morals, and Society.* New York: Viking Press, 1961. Includes an analysis of the social and psychological reasons for war.

FRANK, SUSAN. Interview with E. B. White. *Cornell Daily Sun* (October 9, 1964), pp. S2, S8. Good interview; contains much information about his Cornell days.

―――. "White Enjoys Relaxed Climate with Picturesque View of Bay," *Cornell Daily Sun* (October 9, 1964), p. S2. Short comment about White to accompany interview.

FULLER, J. W. "Prose Style in the Essays of E. B. White." University of Washington, 1959. Unpublished dissertation. Excellent, exhaustive analysis of White's prose style.

GEISMAR, MAXWELL. *Writers in Crisis.* Boston: Houghton Mifflin Co., 1942. Literature during the 1930's: American writers gain in stature through the crisis of the depression.

"Go Climb a More Meaningful Tree," *The Commonweal,* LI (March 10, 1950), 573. One of the few negative reviews of White's work.

GOLD, HERBERT. " 'The Points of My Compass: Letters from the East, the West, the North, the South,' by E. B. White," *Saturday Review,* XLV (November 24, 1962), 30. Notes the importance of Thoreau for an understanding of White. Mildly critical of what he regards as White's restraint, lack of emotion.

GURKO, LEO. *The Angry Decade.* New York: Dodd, Mead & Co., 1947. Literary and cultural background of the 1930's; suggests De Voto was wrong in his *The Literary Fallacy;* speaks of the importance of *The New Yorker* in the 1930's. But see below.

————. *Heroes, Highbrows and the Popular Mind.* Indianapolis: Bobbs-Merrill Co., Inc., 1953. Contains some sharp comments about *The New Yorker*—calls it "a brilliant monument to negativism."

HARRIMAN, MARGARET CASE. *The Vicious Circle: The Story of the Algonquin Round Table.* New York: Rinehart & Co., 1951. Account of a lively group of New Yorkers; White was not one of them.

HASLEY, LOUIS. "The Talk of the Town and the Country: E. B. White," *Connecticut Review,* V (October, 1971), 37-45. An appreciative, pleasant survey of White's work, with emphasis on "The Morning of the Day They Did It."

HENTOFF, NAT. "Tom Wolfe and *The New Yorker*," *The Village Voice,* X (May 6, 1965), 5, 10. Contains some remarks about the freedom *The New Yorker* gives to its writers.

HOFFMAN, FREDERICK J. *The Twenties.* New York: Collier Books, 1962. Fine analysis of American culture of the decade.

HOUGHTON, DONALD E. *"The New Yorker:* Exponent of a Cosmopolitan Elite." University of Minnesota, 1955. Unpublished dissertation. Good, objective, favorable account of *The New Yorker;* lacks partisan flavor of some published accounts.

HYMAN, STANLEY EDGAR. "The Urban New Yorker," *The New Republic,* CVII (July 20, 1942), 90-92. Valuable comments on *The New Yorker;* stresses importance of White and "Notes and Comment"; rejects notion that *The New Yorker* has a fixed tone or attitude.

[INGERSOLL, RALPH]. *"The New Yorker,"* Fortune, X (August, 1934), 72-86, 90, 92, 97, 150, 152. One of the good, early accounts of *The New Yorker;* contains some inaccuracies about salaries.

KRAMER, DALE. *Ross and the New Yorker.* Garden City: Doubleday & Co., 1951. Best published account of the magazine; information on E. B. White, Katharine White, James Thurber, and Wolcott Gibbs, as well as Ross.

KRUTCH, JOSEPH WOOD. "The Profession of a New Yorker," *The Saturday Review of Literature*, XXXVII (January 30, 1954), 15-16. Review of *The Second Tree from the Corner*; some comments about White and *The New Yorker*.

MALONEY, RUSSELL. "Tilley the Toiler," *The Saturday Review of Literature*, XXX (August 30, 1947), 7-10, 29-32. Discussion of White's role as a writer of "Notes and Comment" in *The New Yorker*; stresses the importance of Thurber and White.

McCORD, DAVID. *Yale Review*, XXVIII (December, 1928), 392-394. Favorable, perceptive review of White's poetry.

MEYER, CORD JR. *Peace or Anarchy*. Boston: Little, Brown & Co., 1943. Like *The Wild Flag*, a plea for world unity.

MORRIS, WRIGHT. *The Territory Ahead*. New York: Harcourt, Brace & Co., 1957. Study of nostalgia in certain American writers from Thoreau to Faulkner.

MOWRY, GEORGE E. (ed.). *The Twenties*. Englewood Cliffs: Prentice-Hall, 1963. Collection of contemporary articles on the 1920's.

MURRAY, ROBERT K. *Red Scare*. Minneapolis: University of Minnesota Press, 1955. Good account of the anti-Communist mania in the 1920's.

NORDELL, RODERICK. "The Writer as a Private Man," *Christian Science Monitor* (October 31, 1962) p. 9. One of the rare interviews with E. B. White; informative about his private life.

REVES, EMERY. *The Anatomy of Peace*. New York: Pocket Books, 1946. One of the early and most popular appeals for world federation.

SCHOTT, WEBSTER. "E. B. White Forever," *The New Republic*, CXLVII (November 24, 1962), 23-24. Sharply critical review of *The Points of My Compass*: sees White as restrained, urbane, and preoccupied with minor matters.

SHENKER, ISRAEL. "E. B. White: Notes and Comment by Author," *The New York Times* (July 11, 1969), pp. 31, 43. Most recent comment in print about White; notes that he finds it hard to write now, even letters.

SMITH, J. THORNE. "Advertising." *Civilization in the United States*, ed. Harold Stearns. New York: Harcourt, Brace & Co., 1922. Perceptive and sensitive article.

STEARNS, HAROLD (ed.). *America Now*. New York: Charles Scribner's Sons, 1938. Contains useful articles on various aspects of American culture; includes one on advertising by Roy Durstine.

———. (ed.). *Civilization in the United States.* New York: Harcourt, Brace, & Co., 1922. Collection of articles on American culture.

STEINHOFF, WILLIAM R. " 'The Door': 'The Professor,' 'My Friend the Poet (Deceased),' 'The Washable House,' and 'The Man Out in Jersey,' " *College English,* XXIII (December, 1961), 229-32. One of the rare, and good, critical articles on a work by E. B. White. Relates the story to contemporary events.

SWING, RAYMOND GRAM. *Forerunners of American Fascism.* New York: Julian Messner, 1935. Good account of people like Father Coughlin and Gerald L. K. Smith.

THOMAS, SIDNEY SAMUEL. *"The New Yorker's* Contributions to the Book World During a Quarter Century." University of Georgia, 1950. Unpublished master's thesis. Thorough account of books first published in part or in full in *The New Yorker.*

THURBER, JAMES. "E. B. W.," *The Saturday Review of Literature,* XVIII (October 15, 1938), 8-9. Appreciative, witty comment by one of White's close friends. Mentions White's favorite books, his half-serious fear of death, his sensitivity, and so on; considerable information about White on *The New Yorker.*

———. *The Years with Ross.* Boston: Little, Brown & Co., 1959. More personal account than Dale Kramer's; both necessary in understanding *The New Yorker.*

VAN GELDER, ROBERT. *Writers and Writing.* New York: Charles Scribner's Sons, 1946. Contains an appreciative interview with White.

WALKER, STANLEY. "Books," *New York Herald Tribune* (October 21, 1962), p. 5. Praises White as an essayist; finds value and strength in White's restraint.

WEATHERBY, W. J. "A Modern Man of Walden," *Manchester Guardian Weekly* (February 14, 1963), p. 14. Interview with E. B. White; focuses on White's relationship to Thoreau.

*Index*

# Index

*Index* [ 189 ]

Updike, John, 162
"Urban New Yorker," 64
Uruguay, 61
U-2 incident, 136

Van Gelder, Robert, 64
*Van Zanten's Happy Days*, 57
Viet Nam, 42, 84, 134, 135, 138, 150
Voice of America, 149
Voltaire, 114

*Walden*, see Thoreau, Henry
*Wanderer*, 57
"Was Lifted by Ears as a Boy, No
  Harm Done," 128
Watt, William W., 78
*Wave of the Future*, 71, 72-74
Weatherby, W. J., 154
Webster, Daniel, 69
Wells, H. G., 83-84
*What Are We to Do with Our Lives?*,
  83, 84
White, E. B., childhood, adoles-
  cence, 128, 129; earliest writing,
  19; college, 19-27; Students Army
  Training Corps, 21; courses at
  college, 21; *Sun* editorials, 22-27;
  prize for editorial, 23; brief jobs
  after college, 27-28; across coun-
  try in Model T, 28-29; job on
  Seattle *Times*, 29-31, 112; Alaska,
  28, 31-33; first years in New York
  City, 33-36, 112; beginning work
  with *The New Yorker*, 35-37, 112;
  marriage, 37, 41, 129; birth of
  son, 41; starts full-time on *New
  Yorker*, 49; leaves New York for
  Maine, 64-66; returns to New

York, 77, 81-82; at U.N. Confer-
  ence in San Francisco, 87-89; Post
  W.W.II, 106; reduces contribu-
  tions to *New Yorker*, 131; returns
  to Maine, 132
White, Joel, 41, 74, 75, 76, 77, 129
White, Katharine S., 50, 77, 95, 131-
  32, 133, 144, 155, 161. See also
  Angell, Katharine S.
White, Lee Strout, 61
Whitman, Walt, 39, 46
Wienkus, Mrs., 113
*Wild Flag*, 50, 61, 68, 77, 81-93, 97,
  134, 136, 137, 151
Wilkie, Wendell, 85
"Will Strunk," 151
Wilson, Edmund, 60, 162
*Wind in the Willows*, 95, 99
"Window Box," 40
Winnie the Pooh, 95
Winrod, Gerald B., 73
Wintman, Captain, 89
WLBZ (Bangor, Maine), 149
Woollcott, Alexander, 36
Wordsworth, William, 39
"World of Tomorrow," 71
*World of William Clissold*, 83
World Peaceways, 85
"Writer as a Private Man," 65
*Writers and Writing*, 64

"Years of Wonder," 28, 31, 32, 33,
  130, 147-48, 160
*Years with Ross*, 49, 132
Yeats, W. B., 40, 46

"Zoo Revisited," 20, 125, 126-30,
  147

| DATE DUE | | | |
|---|---|---|---|
| | | | |
| | | | |
| | | | |
| | | | |
| | | | |
| | | | |
| | | | |
| | | | |
| | | | |
| | | | |
| | | | |
| | | | |
| | | | |
| | | | |
| | | | |
| | | | |
| | | | |
| GAYLORD | | | PRINTED IN U.S.A. |